THE GAME THEY PLAYED

The Game They Played

STANLEY COHEN

FARRAR, STRAUS AND GIROUX • NEW YORK

Library of Congress Cataloging in Publication Data
Cohen, Stanley.
The game they played.
1. Basketball—United States. 2. Sports betting.
3. Bribery—United States. I. Title
GV885.4.C63   1977   364.1'72   77–3710

For Betty, Linda, and Steven

and

for my father

I owe special thanks to Martin Pops, my long-time friend and literary conscience, for his advice, encouragement, and unsparing criticism; Roger W. Straus III, who got me out of the starting gate and offered valued guidance with patience, enthusiasm, and always good cheer; Aaron Asher, who helped me through the stretch and, with a light touch, made the days of completion relatively painless; Angus Cameron, who heard it all from the start and inevitably pointed a finger in the right direction; Seán O Loingsigh, who copy-edited the manuscript with care and discernment; Marty Glickman and Junius Kellogg, who were generous with their time and candid with their comments; the many others, too numerous to mention, who were ready to contribute bits of information and to share their recollections. And finally, to all those quick-guns from the old neighborhood in the Bronx, whose memory brightened my trek through the past.

S.C.

THE GAME THEY PLAYED

PROLOGUE

It was the big man who drew the crowd. He had been gone for a long season and now, in the first true chill of November, he was back, doing the thing he had always done best. He was playing the pivot in a schoolyard basketball game, positioned with his back to the basket and spinning left or right in the brief pirouettes of an unrehearsed choreography.

He was a big man, but he had an unorthodox shape for the game he played. His body seemed to be formed by a succession of sharp hooks and angles, except for the slightly rounded shoulders and the face, which was full and fleshy. His very presence spoke of awkwardness, but in context everything he did acquired the mysterious beauty of function. For there was to his movements the quick stuttering ease, the economy of motion, that is taught in the brightness of the big time but is refined and finally possessed in the lonely litanies of the schoolyard dusk.

The crowd had gathered slowly. They were clustered in a tight semicircle around the back of the basket, drawn in almost directly beneath the backboard. It was late in the day, and beyond the crossed wire fence, some six feet above the playing surface, twilight figures moved like shadows in the direction of the five- and six-story tenements that lined both sides of the street. Except for this one small corner, the schoolyard was empty now, and it was quiet. The only sounds to be heard were the sounds of the game itself, the ball drumming against the concrete court, or rattling against the rim or the metal backboard.

There were five other players on the court. The big man was being guarded by a player of perhaps six feet two, who was giving away almost four inches in height. But he was quick and lean and very agile, and as one watched him the impression grew that his body had been wired together with catgut and whipcord. He wore a close-cropped crew cut, which was the fashion of the time, and his soft, almost casual jump shots were flicked lightly from the top of his head. The two had very different playing styles, one seemingly set against the other in the practiced medley of counterpoint.

The remaining four players formed the supporting cast. They had their own skills, some of them considerable, and on other days one or another might have stolen the game, but not today. This day, they all seemed to understand, was special because the big man was back. And so they played to the strength of his inside game, feeding the pivot and then cutting across, fast and tight, like spokes slicing past the hub of a wheel.

The pace of the game was swift and precise. The big man's team scored the first three baskets. He made the first two himself on two short spin shots, one to his right, the other to his left. On the next play he passed off for a driving lay-up. Then a shot was missed, and the crew-cut player answered back with two jump shots, fired in a flat trajectory that appeared to be short of the basket, but somehow just cleared the top and grazed the inside of the back rim before falling to the ground.

There were no nets on the baskets, and as the afternoon faded the rim seemed to lose itself against the green of the backboard. But schoolyard basketball is a game played on the accumulated instincts of one's own time and place. There were no markings on the court; no keyhole or foul line, and one learned to take his points of reference from anonymous landmarks—a jagged crack in the pavement, an imperceptible dip in the wall along the sideline, the subtle geography that is known and stored only in the private preserve of the body.

Three-man basketball is conceivably the most demanding game played in the schoolyards of America. It is not as sophisticated as the full-court game. It does not require the same kind of speed or versatility, the almost artistic devotion to discipline. But what it lacks in complexity is compensated by the intense quality of the game. It is pressure basketball, compacted in time and space, as if a boxing match were to be held in a ring cut to half its normal size. There is no place to hide and no clock to offer respite.

The game is played by the improvised rules of the home court. In some neighborhoods ten baskets win a game, in others the point is eight, but always a two-basket, or four-point, margin is required for victory. It is a game played to its own cadence, and without a referee to call fouls, it can be brutally tough. But the most important feature of three-man basketball is that the team that scores keeps possession of the ball, and so one plays always with the nagging knowledge that the game might be lost without his ever having had the chance to score. It is a shooter's game, a game that is won or lost quickly on the trigger of the hottest gun.

Now, from the corner of the court, the big man sent up a one-hand push shot that cut the center of the rim so cleanly that one could not be certain it had gone through. It broke a 10–10 tie, and before the defensive team could recover, another shot, as whistling clean as the first, fell through from slightly closer range, and the game was one basket short of completion. They were the first outside shots the big man had made, and now one recalled how easily he had made those shots, and how often, on brighter nights, beneath the hundred blazing suns of big-city arenas.

That was a while ago of course, and a long season had passed since those days of early spring in 1950 when time seemed to move on private clocks, and each night was a herald to the sound of trumpets. He was not yet twenty then, a college sophomore with honors for grades and a basketball talent that might earn him All-American mention. He had not played much basketball until he reached high school, and his natural gifts were modest. He had size, of course, and good hands, and a remarkably soft touch from the outside. But the rest of it was learned. It was learned while in high school, and then honed and polished in the schoolyards of the Bronx. He worked hard at it, shooting at night-darkened rims, and in winter clearing a path through the snow so that his shooting eye would not lose its edge. Basketball was a sport without season in the canyons of New York, and the big man, who had grown to love the game, worked at it through the months and years of his teens.

He was all-scholastic in high school, and in college he joined four other all-scholastic players on a freshman squad that could have taken the measure of more than a few college varsities. A year later they moved up as a unit to a team that was deep in talent. It was a team marked early for greatness, but no one, not even its most optimistic fans and alumni, suspected that by season's end this young racehorse band of schoolyard players would beat the best the country had to offer and win both of America's major college tournaments.

They had become instant celebrities, their fame of a type seldom known to professional athletes. For they were, after all, college kids, none yet old enough to vote, and they were the local property of the neighborhoods in which they lived. It was not through bubble-gum cards or the filter of the television screen that you knew them. You would see them on the block, or at the corner candy store, and of course in the schoolyard where you would watch them play in street clothes on the Sunday after a game, and on occasion, if the available talent was skimpy that day, you might even share the court with one of them in a three-man game.

The big man was a schoolyard regular. He would arrive late on a Sunday morning, sometimes carrying a basketball under his arm, and he would shoot at an open basket while waiting his turn to take the court. He was genial and unassuming, and even on the day after his team had won the National Invitation Tournament, he came to play choose-up ball, and as he entered the schoolyard he received the applause with a diffident grace.

It had all seemed right then. The days fell together with brickwork precision, and time was the filament on which success was measured. There was not the slightest intimation then that a year later his well-ordered world of campus and schoolyard would lay in ruin. Other glories waited; the NCAA championship would be added to the NIT title within the next two weeks, but further on, around the bend of the seasons, lay the wreckage of a national scandal. He and some of his teammates would be arrested for manipulating the scores of basketball games. They would be booked on charges of bribery and conspiracy, they would be arraigned, bail would be set, they would be convicted and sentenced. Some would receive jail terms. That is what lay ahead, eleven months to the day, and that was not necessarily the worst of it.

The worst of it, they would find, was that forgiveness would be slow. They would be remembered more widely as dumpers than as the celebrated grand-slam team. Careers would be broken, their educations stunted. They would never again play big-time basketball. Culture heroes in their teens, by the time they turned twenty they would be part of the dark side of American folklore. And it would not be short-lived. Twenty-five years later their telephone numbers would still be unlisted. They were to learn something soon about one of life's fundamental truths, as relentless as it is just: that the past is not neutral; it takes revenge.

Now, as you watched him again, you had to wonder what it all meant for him, you would like to know how much of it he understood now that the legalities were done, now that he was free to do anything except what he really wanted to do. You imagined the inside of his head to be a kaleidoscope of gray-green colors, of pictures that fed one into the other, whipping like wind through the tunnels of memory. And you wondered where it might stop, which frame might be frozen in view even now, as the ball snapped into the pivot, into the hands held high above the head, the ball raised like a torch against the dusk.

He stayed that way, motionless, for an instant, his back to the basket, the ball held high. Then he started to turn quickly to his right, his head and shoulders doing all of the work, and as quickly he was spinning the other way now, spinning left, the ball balanced lightly on the tips of his fingers, his arm stretching high toward the right side of the basket, and then the ball, in the air now, struck the crease between the rim and the backboard and bounced away, out of bounds.

And then something happened. It happened so quickly that it all seemed at the time to blur into the bleakness of imagination. But it would be recalled later in the finest of detail, summoned forth as if it had all taken place in slow motion to be run at will in the instant replay of the mind.

Two copper pennies were thrown out onto the court. They were tossed at the same time, in the same motion, and they hit one in back of the other with the abrupt report of two shots fired from a pistol. You heard them hit that way, and then you saw them roll briefly and fall, and then they were lying right beneath the basket, at the big man's feet.

The game stopped now, and everyone was looking in the direction of a boy of perhaps fifteen or sixteen. He was of medium build, and he was wearing a brown suede zipper jacket above faded blue jeans. He was smiling now, a tentative smile, as if to assure that no malice was intended, but he said nothing. He said nothing and you could hear the silence as the crew-cut jump shooter walked toward the youth. He was just a few steps away, and he walked up to him matter-of-factly and with his left hand he seized the kid by the front of the jacket, and without saying a word he eased him back in the direction of the wall.

Then, with a quick short motion, he punched out with his right hand and landed hard and clean against the side of the youth's face. You could hear the sound of the punch landing and then the kid's head bouncing lightly against the black metal door, and nothing else. The kid did not even cry out. All you heard was a muffled groan, almost inaudible, the type that follows a blow to the body. But the punch had landed flush, and the kid, making hardly a sound, sagged to the single step at the base of the door. He said nothing, and for a moment you could hardly believe it had happened.

But when the kid picked himself up you could see that his jaw was hanging loose. His jaw was dangling as if from a swivel, and on the left side of his face, where the blow had struck, there was a lump that jutted out and up in the direction of his ear. It was not the puffed-out swelling that comes with a bruise. It was, clearly, the sharp impression of a splintered bone pushing against the inside of his cheek.

The jump shooter had turned away, even before the youth drew himself up, and he walked slowly back to the court. He stopped beneath the basket, at the in-bounds line, and he waited.

"Your ball," the big man said.

PART ONE

They had played the game with a careless elegance, with the arrogant street smarts of the New York slick. Their skills were polished in the hardwood corridors of the city's schools, but the magic, the quick pickpocket swagger of their hustler's style, was acquired in the playgrounds and schoolyards of a city in which the game of basketball is less a sport than a sacrament.

In a way, they belonged to New York more than any other team in any other sport, more even than the Brooklyn Dodgers of the same era, more than the Yankees or the Giants or the New York Knicks. For they were not aliens who came to the city for the duration of a season, only to return to the yawning plains of middle America or the sweet slow rhythms of the South when the season was done. There were no foreign addresses among them, there was no twang or drawl to their speech, no farm-boy shuffle to their gait, none of the wide-eyed, small-town innocence that craned its neck at tall buildings or dreamed of leaves burning in the backyards of October.

They were, all of them, street kids from the pavements of New York, from the sullen ghettos of Harlem and Brooklyn and the Bronx. They learned to play basketball three men to a side in the half-court corners of the neighborhood schoolyards, shooting at warped rims and metal backboards. It was a city game played by makeshift city rules and governed by the imperative that only the winner gets to stay for dessert. The protocol was unspoken, but it never varied. The winning team would hold the court for as long as it won, and the losers left in favor of three new challengers. Defeat, therefore, carried with it an air of finality. It was not unlike competing in a major college tournament; you had to win to keep playing.

Some of the best basketball players in America passed through those schoolyards, received their first real coaching in high school, and were recruited by big-time colleges across the nation. They went to basketball factories like Kentucky or Bradley, where their tuition and living expenses were paid so long as they made the team. Many stayed in New York, on scholarships from NYU, Long Island University, or St. John's. Some—those who could meet the academic requirements—enrolled at City College, the College of the City of New York, where tuition was free, athletes were granted no favors, and basketball was coached by Nat Holman. In the fall of 1948, Ed Warner, Ed Roman, Floyd Layne, Al Roth, and Herb Cohen—all products of New York City high schools—entered City College and formed perhaps the finest freshman team the school had ever had. A year later they moved up to the varsity, and together with two seniors—Irwin Dambrot and Norman Mager—they comprised the core of the 1949–50 City College grand-slam team, the only college basketball team ever to win both the National Invitation Tournament and the NCAA championship in the same season. It was a unique team by big-time college standards. Four members of the starting five—Warner, Roman, Layne, and Roth—were sophomores. All, of course, were New York City residents and, it was presumed, all had met the rigid academic qualifications; they had not been solicited for their skills.

By season's end, their accomplishments would be legend. They would win seven consecutive post-season games from carefully molded teams representing the basketball emporiums of San Francisco, Kentucky, Duquesne, Ohio State, North Carolina State, and

Bradley twice. Bradley was rated the number-one team in the country and was top-seeded in both tournaments. The nationwide poll of the Associated Press ranked Ohio State second, Kentucky third, North Carolina State fifth, and Duquesne sixth. San Francisco, the only team not included in the top ten, was the defending NIT champion. The City team had little to recommend it. The national poll placed it in a tie with Vanderbilt for twenty-seventh place, and it was rated a seven-to-one underdog against the nation's heavyweights. But the New Yorkers beat them all, in straight sets. They won with the New York City type of basketball—break fast and bust for home—with big-city style and cool, with the finely honed instincts of the streets and the schoolyards, the grim certain knowledge that you had to win to keep the court.

The double tourney sweep was an upset of dimensions not easily measured. No team is ever a favorite to win seven straight games against its peers. Basketball is a game of subtle and various rhythms; its possibilities are infinite. It does not run to form as truly as football, where power tends to assert itself in the course of sixty minutes. College basketball is the game of the forty-minute hour, and a team that runs out to an early lead can slow the pace and keep its opponent from gaining access to the ball. It is the only sport in which a team, theoretically, can remain on offense without trying to score and is never required to relinquish its right to possession.

The styles and strategies of the two opposing teams therefore can be as vital to the outcome of a game as their relative merits. Speed can be neutralized by a patterned attack; a height advantage can be nullified by a zone defense; and a full-court press can break the tempo of the hottest shooting team. In the course of two consecutive tournaments a team will be forced to improvise. It will be called upon to adjust spontaneously to a network of strategies no less complex than those employed in a chess match, and there is little time for contemplation. It is an adage of sports that the hot team will win a short series, but that is a random measure. It has some validity for a series in which two teams play only one another. There, the team that wins the first game, or the first two, musters a psychological advantage. It enters the next contest with the attitude of a winner, and the other side must ponder the likelihood that it is simply outclassed.

But an elimination tournament is more exacting. Every team that takes the court arrives a winner. The teams that play in the finals are undefeated in tourney play. It takes something special to win that kind of competition. What is required is a witch's brew of poise, tenacity, a degree of character, a sense of destiny, and the unbreakable conviction that there is no contingency for which it is unprepared. It is not the hot team that wins such a tournament; it is the team that is ready.

There were few who believed that City College was suited to the task. The team was inexperienced, it lacked real height, it had been erratic throughout the regular season. In fact, the season closed as something of a disappointment. City had been expected to be the best of the metropolitan teams, rated slightly ahead of LIU and St. John's. It had a solid corps of returning veterans which would be nourished by the freshman five of the previous season. The team was so rich in talent that Nat Holman began the season by experimenting with a two-platoon system. He established two separate fives, each a mix of sophomores and lettermen, with the intention of using them as individual units until he found the proper blend. There was no one with a surer eye for basketball talent than Nat Holman, and he knew from the outset that he was staked to something special this season. Still, he was cautious in his appraisal of the team. He was counting heavily on a group of newcomers, and he understood that even the best freshman credentials often turned to counterfeit under the lights of the big time.

And so Holman hedged his bets. He opened the season with a starting five consisting of two seniors and three sophs. Roth and Mike Wittlin, a senior, were paired in the backcourt; Warner teamed with the veteran Dambrot at forwards; and Roman started at center. City was quick off the mark. After an easy warm-up victory over Queens College, it made its Madison Square Garden debut against Lafayette, and won by thirty-two points. Already the cast of the future was indicated. Four of the five top scorers were sophomores. Roman was high with eighteen points, Cohen scored thirteen, Roth had nine, and Warner and Wittlin each scored eight. But what impressed most was the speed and sureness with which the team played. Covering the game for *The New York Times,* Lou Effrat wrote:

"They do things, these Beavers. They do them knowingly and they do them well. So well, in fact, that at times last night it became difficult to follow their progress. The Lavender is loaded."

The next three games were track meets for the Beavers. They breezed past Southern Methodist, Kings Point, and Brooklyn College by margins of twelve, fifty-four, and twenty-seven points, and the sophomores continued to assert themselves with Warner, Roman, and Roth taking turns as high scorer, abetted by Dambrot, who achieved double figures in each of the games. It was at this point that Holman made a change in his starting lineup. He replaced Wittlin at guard with Floyd Layne, a wiry, gangling defensive specialist who, for the balance of the season, would remain in the starting five.

The debut of the new unit was less than auspicious. It played poorly against a seasoned, methodical Oklahoma team, unable to cope with the Sooners' double-screen offense, and took its first loss of the season by a score of 67–63. The Beavers bounced back with an easy win over California, and then stumbled again, losing their last game of 1949 to a strong UCLA team by seven points. The first game of the new year would be a pivotal one for CCNY. Its opponent would be St. John's University, which at that point in the season, almost halfway through its schedule, was rated the number-one team in the country.

St. John's was undefeated in its first twelve games. It had beaten top-ranked Kentucky, the NCAA champions, by eleven points, and two games later won even more handily over San Francisco, winners of the NIT. City, with its six-and-two record, had beaten no one of national stature. Holman, obviously looking for additional experience in the backcourt, restored Wittlin to the starting lineup in place of Al Roth, and the strategy worked well at the outset. The first half might have been given as a clinic in schoolyard basketball. The

Beavers appeared to be carried on pockets of air as they glided up and down the court, the ball passed from one to the other as if controlled by a puppeteer's strings. They whirled and turned in swift ballets of motion, their shots almost anticlimactic, like the clash of cymbals fitted to the nuance of the maestro's baton. City led by 27–18 at the half.

But now another move was in order. Holman decided to go the entire second half with his five sophomores. Roth and Cohen were in for Dambrot and Wittlin. And this move too seemed blessed. City increased its lead to fifteen points, 41–26, with thirteen minutes left to play. But then the close-kept rhythm of the game was broken. City began to freeze the ball, trying to run out the clock, and it was in the precise patterns of the clock-killing weave that the team's youth and inexperience began to pick at the fabric of its style. They turned the ball over, they had it stolen, and St. John's, with patience and care, narrowed the margin to two points at 50–48. Then Roman, working from the pivot, fed Warner, who drove by Al McGuire and twisted his way to the basket. Now, with time running out, the teams were trading baskets, and with City ahead 54–51, St. John's had a chance to win the game in the very last seconds. Ronnie MacGilvray drove in looking for a three-point play—a basket and a foul—and as he let go his shot Roth fouled him. But the shot bounced off the rim as the buzzer sounded, and MacGilvray stepped to the line for two meaningless free throws. He made the first and missed the second, and City had a two-point decision. Roman scored twenty-three points, and Warner seventeen, which is to say they accounted for forty of the team's fifty-four points, and even more remarkably they scored all but four of City's points in the second half.

The St. John's game established the character of the City team. Now it had defeated the best in the country. It had done it with sophomores. It had clung to a narrow lead and withstood the most intense pressure. To its natural assets of speed and precision was now added a measure of poise. And the one-two punch of Roman and Warner had shone brightly. Roman played head to head with Bob (Zeke) Zawoluk, the gifted St. John's center, and outscored him.

Warner played even more brilliantly. His points were made against Al McGuire, a tenacious defender, and he displayed a quickness and a magic of moves subtle enough for the classical stage.

Still, not all of the critics were convinced. The national AP poll continued to rank St. John's first in the country, followed by Kentucky and yet another metropolitan team, LIU. City was rated no better than seventh, and it would never climb higher. But the Beavers were not concerned with the polls. They had acquired something in the game with St. John's. It was more than just confidence. They had, in a sense, for the first time that season, gained possession of themselves.

City won its next six games, by margins as great as twenty-five points. The team seemed to bring its talents to their peak against West Virginia, dazzling the Madison Square Garden crowd with multiple passes and combination plays that added up to an 80–55 victory. It ascended to even greater heights a week later against Muhlenberg. The Beavers ran up a total of ninety-five points, an astounding figure in 1950. Roman scored twenty-seven points, twenty of them in the first half, and he was followed by Warner with eighteen, Cohen with sixteen, and Dambrot with eleven.

Holman called it the team's best game of the season. It was the first of five consecutive road games, and City showed that it knew more than one route to the winner's circle. It staked Boston College to an early lead, and then roared from behind in the last ten minutes with Roman and Warner leading the closing drive to an eight-point decision. Against Princeton, champions of the Ivy League, City was stalled by a pressing zone defense that held it to twenty-three points in the first half. But the Beavers went to a fast break after intermission and cracked the game open without benefit of an outside shot. It was Nat Holman's 500th game as City College coach, and it was followed four days later by a victory over St. Francis to run the midseason winning streak to seven.

Then the team began to falter. A last-minute outburst against Canisius fell short, and the return to the Garden brought no better luck. Favored by more than ten points against a swift Niagara team,

City played its worst game of the season and lost 68–61. So frantically precise during the winning streak, moving as if to medleys only they could hear, the Beavers seemed a different team against Niagara. It was more than just a poor game. It appeared, rather, to be a fall from grace, as if they had lost favor with a deity that had nurtured and guarded their cause.

Neither Canisius nor Niagara had imposing credentials. St. John's had disposed of both of them, by twelve and nine points, just two days before they defeated City. Holman said that his team had gone sour. It fell to thirteenth in the national ratings, and the slide continued despite decisions over St. Joseph's and Fordham in the next two games. For even in victory, the team no longer impressed. Its fast break sputtered, its ball handling had become slovenly, its shooting sporadic. It had never been, after all, an overpowering team, but one built on the most delicate scales of balance and precision. It won with finesse. Now, it appeared, there was sand in the gears, as though someone had tampered, just a bit, with the most finely tuned machine.

The Beavers blew open the St. Joseph's game in three furious minutes of the second half, and they skidded even closer to the brink against Fordham, winning with a seven-point burst in the final three and a half minutes. The team seemed to have lost its ability to dominate a game, to control its tempo. Instead, it counted on quick flurries to overcome extended periods of disarray, much like an aging boxer who hoards his energy for the last minute of each round. It was a technique that worked only against outclassed opponents. It failed against Syracuse.

Syracuse was a team that was constructed on the element of speed, and it challenged City at its own game, a strategy that had worked for both UCLA and Niagara. This time the closing drive fell short. City cut nine points from a ten-point lead in the last six minutes, but the effort drained the last of the team's resources. Syracuse responded with eight points of its own and won by a comfortable nine-point margin.

Three days later, the first three bids to the National Invitation

Tournament were accepted by St. John's, Bradley, and Duquesne. Ohio State, rated second in the country behind Bradley, and Holy Cross, undefeated in twenty-five games and ranked third, accepted invitations to play in the NCAA. City was no longer listed among the top thirty teams in the nation, and the chance for tournament play seemed lost unless the team could rally in its last two regular-season games, against a pair of metropolitan rivals, Manhattan College and NYU.

City entered the Manhattan game favored by seven and a half points, and it fired out to an eleven-point lead. Then, as though following script, the team slumped and Manhattan drew even in the second half and stayed close until Warner converted a three-point play in the final minute. Even then, the game was not out of reach. Roth threw the ball away on a fast break, and Hank Poppe fed Mike Joyce to bring Manhattan within two points. City had the ball but could not hold it, and Manhattan was staked to no less than five scoring opportunities in the last twenty seconds but failed each time. The Beavers won the game 57–55, but their erratic pattern of play persisted. They continued to be frivolous with a lead. It was no different against NYU. City again was a heavy favorite, and again it moved ahead, this time by twelve points, and again it allowed the lead to slip away, falling six points behind midway through the second half. It took a late drive, sparked by two quick Roth baskets, and a precarious last-minute freeze to assure a three-point victory.

City ended its season with a record of seventeen and five and received one of the last three bids to the NIT. But the team had not played a solid game of basketball in a month, and it seemed ill prepared for the rigors of tournament play. Nat Holman was not optimistic.

"I hope we can justify the invitation," he said, and he immediately began taking inventory. The team had been beaten five times during the season, and a variety of weaknesses had been exposed. In its first loss, City had been unable to switch defensive assignments against Oklahoma's screen plays, often leaving a man open for a shot. UCLA, a quick team, used a collapsing defense, blocking the lanes to the

• 21

basket and forcing the Beavers to shoot from beyond their normal range of effectiveness. Canisius had won by carefully controlling the pace of the game, taking an early lead and then slowing the tempo. Niagara simply outran them and beat them off the boards, and Syracuse employed a combination of speed and precise outside shooting.

But the Syracuse loss had done something for City as well. It had, it turned out, provided Holman with a new weapon, uncovered by chance when Ed Roman, the bruising six-foot-six center, fouled out of the game after scoring twenty-three points. Ed Warner, some three inches shorter than Roman, was shifted from his forward position to the pivot. By every reasonable standard, Warner was not big enough to play center for a major college team. But he was a consummate athlete, gifted with a body that was molded to classic lines. He was lean and quick and fluid in his movements. It appeared, at times, as if he were moving in three directions at once, starting left with his back to the basket, then faking right, and turning back again, moving to his left, sliding between two defenders, slithering toward the basket with the soft easy grace of a cat skimming a tightrope, changing pace and direction in midcourse as he sprang toward the hoop, the ball locked in his sure, long-fingered hands, the arc toward the basket slow and precise, nuzzling the glass of the backboard before dropping through. Warner adapted to the new position immediately. He was high scorer in each of the last two games, with sixteen points against Manhattan and twenty-six against NYU, a record for a City College player in Madison Square Garden.

With Warner in the bucket, Roman moved to a corner position, where he was no less effective. Roman, who could score with either hand from the inside, had, from the outside, the shooting touch of a small man. He sent up one-hand push shots from off his right shoulder with the light practiced touch of the schoolyard sharp. One could see, even from behind the basket, the slow backward rotation of the seams as the ball started its journey from hand to hoop, not launched but pushed into space from twenty feet away, describing the measured parabola that is the first geometric truth for anyone who has ever played the game, and then falling to target, splitting the rim at its center, and brushing past the cords of the basket with that faint swishing sound, the quick short whoosh, that is background music to a thousand boyhood dreams.

Roman continued to start at center, but the two players shuttled in and out of the pivot as the progress and strategy of each game dictated. An opposing team, falling back on defense, would not know which formation it might encounter, and the man guarding Warner would often be unaccustomed to playing defense from the pivot position. And so City came up to the NIT in much the same fashion as a racehorse that had finished uncertainly its last few times out, but that had discovered in the process a new resource of power and strength. It could unnerve the opposition by running counter to form.

The National Invitation Tournament was considered the world series of collegiate basketball in the forties and early fifties. The sport had taken its first step toward status two days before the end of 1934, when the first of eight regularly scheduled doubleheaders was played at Madison Square Garden. These were the creation of Ned Irish, then a sports writer for the *New York World-Telegram*. Irish was one of a group of sports writers asked by New York's Mayor James J. Walker in 1931 to set up a college basketball program to raise money for those left jobless by the Depression. Six New York colleges performed in a tripleheader on Christmas Eve before a capacity crowd at the Garden, and similar programs drew equally well the next two winters. Irish learned something from the experience. In 1934 he quit his newspaper job to become a full-time basketball promoter. The eight playing dates that season attracted almost one hundred thousand paying customers at a time when most citizens were measuring available funds against the demands of food, rent, and winter clothing.

The game had emerged from the cocoon of the campus gym, and now it was being drawn, inexorably, to the light of the big time. There had been few intersectional games prior to 1935 because teams could not afford the cost of transportation. But with the Garden covering expenses and funneling a portion of the gate back into the college coffers, teams from all over the country came to New York to play basketball in the towering arena in midtown Manhattan. The city again was a melting pot, welcoming the diverse styles and cadences of the Midwest, the South, and the Pacific Coast. Gangling kids from backwater towns would come for a day or two to the Big Apple, to gaze upward at this vertical, gyrating roller coaster of a city, to ride the subways, and walk on Times Square, and eat a meal in a Broadway bistro, and then return home to the corner drugstore in Portland, or Tulsa, or Peoria, Illinois, to tell what it was like to play ball in the Garden.

The Garden became something of a showcase, an experimental laboratory where new forms of play were tested against the traditional —the slow, patterned floor game that ended in a two-hand set shot or a driving lay-up. In December 1936, Stanford University came cross-country from California to challenge Long Island University's forty-three-game winning streak. Stanford was led by Hank Luisetti, whose Wild West one-handed shots captured the attention of New York fans. LIU had its streak snapped, 45–31, and Luisetti's on-the-run shooting style would soon be emulated in schoolyards throughout the city. Only in New York could the best players and teams from all parts of the country be seen, and that diversity became a part of New York basketball. The moves, the shooting techniques, the patterns of play became the nutrient of the schoolyards and the high school gyms, and a kid who could buy his way into Madison Square Garden would select and refine the ingredients that finally would compose his own style of play. It was not accidental, therefore, that for decades to come New York City produced more than its share of the country's best basketball players. New York had become the basketball capital of the nation, and the Garden was its royal palace, a national shrine to every kid who ever staked something of himself on the passage of a ball through a hoop ten feet high.

Intersectional play brought with it an entirely new focus of interest. Did Luisetti's Garden performance indicate a superiority of the wide-open western game over the more disciplined, highly structured play of the East? Could big, rawboned farm boys, their hands toughened at the udder, outmaneuver the slick big-city street kids? A group of New York City sports writers determined that the best way to find out was to stage a post-season invitational tournament to be played, of course, at Madison Square Garden. And so the first NIT was held at the end of the 1937–38 season, with Temple, of Philadelphia, defeating Colorado in the finals.

The following season, the National Collegiate Athletic Association introduced its own tournament, with the teams chosen on the basis of regional conference championships, rather than by invitation, and the final round was held at Evanston, Illinois. But it was the NIT that had the patina. Only the best were invited, and they came to New York to play at the Garden in a series of winner-take-all. The NCAA was decided in whistle-stop towns like Evanston, and for the next three seasons at Kansas City, which was known as Cowtown, USA. Even when the NCAA brought its championship East-West final to the Garden in 1942–43, it still took second billing. The NIT was the original, it was by invitation only, and it was played from start to finish in the Garden, NYC.

The first two National Invitation Tournaments were played with six teams, with the two seeded teams drawing byes and going directly to the semifinals. Beginning with the 1940–41 season, eight teams were invited, and the total grew to twelve in 1948–49. The four seeded teams were granted byes. The remaining eight played an elimination round to determine which would go to the quarterfinals. An unseeded team, therefore, would need four straight victories to win the tournament, and City, of course, was not seeded entering the 1949–50 competition. Drawing opening-round passes were Bradley, the country's number-one-ranked team, followed by Kentucky, Duquesne, and St. John's, rated third, sixth, and ninth in the nation.

The schedule makers matched City against San Francisco in the elimination round, with the winner to meet Kentucky. San Francisco was the Cinderella team of the previous season, which, though unranked, had swept through the opposition. But then the tournament past had been composed largely of upsets. All four seeded teams were eliminated in the quarterfinals. This year the odds makers were looking for form to hold, and with one exception it would.

The San Francisco game was rated even, but right from the start it was no contest at all. The West Coast team appeared to be taken by surprise. City came out running, chewing up the Garden floor in the quick hurried fashion that is known all over the country as New York City basketball. The Beavers led by thirteen at the half, stretched the margin to twenty-two early in the second half, and coasted to a nineteen-point victory. Warner, slipping in and out of the pivot against the much taller Don Lofgran, scored twenty-six points, equaling his record of the previous game, and he and Roman completely controlled the boards. The defense also had been tightened. The Beavers swarmed all over the opposition, stealing the ball and breaking up plays before they could evolve. But the game breaker was Warner, coming into his own now, and Lou Effrat, in a comment that spoke more of the early fifties than of the game itself, noted that rarely had anyone under six foot six so completely dominated a Garden game as "the tricky Negro sophomore ace of the Beavers."

The reckless assault that brought down San Francisco was, it turned out, only a prelude to the game with Kentucky. Kentucky sat at the heights of college basketball during the late forties. The team of the previous year, which won the NCAA tournament after an opening round upset in the NIT, was considered by many the best college team ever to play the game. Four of its starting five—Alex Groza, Ralph Beard, Wah-Wah Jones, and Cliff Barker—were graduated right into a new professional franchise, the Indianapolis Olympians, which in its first year was good enough to win the Western Division title in the NBA. And now, Adolph Rupp, coach of Kentucky and recently named Coach of the Year, was describing his current team in terms of even greater praise.

"This young team of mine," Rupp said, "is better than the group that won the Invitation Tournament as sophomores." That same team had gone to the NIT finals the following year before reaching its peak in 1948–49. Now Rupp had a new cast, an even brighter cast, he thought, and he rated Bill Spivey, his seven-foot center, as superior to Groza at a comparable stage. Spivey, one of the game's first seven-foot giants, was complemented by two returning seniors—Dale Barnstable and Jim Line—and by Walter Hirsch, another returning letterman, and little Bobby Watson in the backcourt.

Kentucky had been favored to sweep both the NIT and the NCAA in 1948–49, but the dream vanished quickly in an opening-round loss to Loyola. Rupp had hoped for a second chance at the unprecedented grand slam this season, but the NCAA bypassed Kentucky in favor of North Carolina State. The NCAA committee contended that Kentucky had turned down the chance to meet North Carolina State in a regional playoff for the spot, but Rupp said he had never received the offer. In any event, the nation's third-ranked team now pinned its claim to national prestige on winning the NIT. It never came close.

CCNY ran Kentucky into the boards, 89–50, in one of the most one-sided games in NIT history. In less than five minutes City had opened a 13–1 lead. Just past the ten-minute mark it was 28–9, and by half time the game stood at 45–20, already out of reach. At one point City scored sixteen straight points in little more than three minutes. Roman, half a foot shorter than Spivey, turned him inside out. He held Spivey to three shots in the first half, maneuvered him into four personal fouls, and both outscored and outrebounded his heralded opponent. Warner, feinting and curling in lay-ups, scored twenty-six points for the third straight game, taking turns with Roman and Al Roth in the pivot. Dambrot silenced Jim Line and scored twenty points himself as City shot a remarkable 45 percent from the floor. It was the worst defeat in Kentucky's forty-six-year history of collegiate basketball.

City had, of course, played inspired, almost perfect basketball, but more important, the team seemed to have found a new level of proficiency. It had steadied itself, it was no longer hitting those dead spots that required last-minute heroics. It had broken out front in both its tournament games and stayed there. It had learned to protect a lead, to treat it with respect. The story was the same against

Duquesne in the semifinals. The Beavers were in control from start to finish, finally winning by a comfortable ten-point margin, and displaying a superbly balanced attack. Warner again was high, this time with nineteen; Roman had fifteen, Layne twelve, Dambrot ten, and Roth chipped in with ten assists. In the nightcap of that Garden doubleheader, Bradley spoiled the chance for an all-New York final by ousting St. John's 83–72, and it would be City against the country's number-one team for the NIT title.

In a rare concession to the demands of an athletic schedule, City College gave its team a day off from classes on the Friday before its clash with Bradley. Holman checked the players into a midtown hotel to keep them together and rested before the game, but some of them —including Dambrot, Layne, and Ronnie Nadell—spent the day at school. Dambrot, who was headed for Columbia Dental School, attended a four-hour physiology lab session and arrived at the hotel late in the afternoon. It was March 17, and Roman, Roth, Cohen, and Mager took the opportunity to walk to Fifth Avenue and watch the St. Patrick's Day parade. When they returned to the hotel, they learned that City had received the District Two bid to the NCAA tournament. The bid had rested on the progress of the NIT. Most observers had expected it to go to St. John's.

Saturday, the day of the game, was a restless time. Holman kept the team together. There would be no individual strolls outside the hotel. The team mapped its strategy and picked its way through the Bradley lineup. Bradley, with a season's record of 26–3, was a curious mixture of size and maneuverability. Elmer Behnke, the six-foot-seven center, Jim Kelly, an inch shorter, and Paul Unruh, the All-American forward, provided the board strength. The running game was led by little Gene Melchiorre, a squat, chunky, five-foot-eight-inch guard who often played the pivot and who was the team's second-leading scorer behind the lanky, almost frail-looking Unruh.

Warner was saying that he would welcome the chance to go against Melchiorre in the pivot, but that job would fall to Layne, who played the most consistent defense for City. Dambrot would guard

Unruh, and Roman would match muscle with Behnke. Those were to be the key match-ups.

The team had an early dinner at the hotel, each player taking an assigned seat at the table in a bow to superstition, and then they went to their rooms to pick up their uniforms. They lingered for a few moments, each dipping into the privacy of his own reserves, and waiting for the first knock on the wall between rooms. The knock, which was traditional, would be passed down the corridor of the hotel, and then the players would leave together, going down through the lobby, and out into the twenty-degree cold of late winter. It was a short walk to Madison Square Garden.

There was a magical quality to the Garden on the night of a big game. The Garden in those days, the old Garden, stood like a medieval fortress on Eighth Avenue between Forty-ninth and Fiftieth streets. The crowd funneled up from under the ground, from the Independent Subway, into the twilight shadow of sport's first great indoor temple. There was a huge theater-type marquee on the Eighth Avenue side, the white background glowing back at the dusk, its message shaped in bold black letters. "NIT Finals," it would read tonight, "CCNY vs Bradley." And you would come up out of the subway and pass under the marquee into an arcade that included a Davega sporting-goods store, a shop that sold Adam hats, and most noted of all, at the right corner of the arcade, there was a Nedick's fast-food counter. Yes, Nedick's was like an extension of the Garden in the forties and fifties. You would meet there before the game for a grilled frank and a World Famous Orange Drink, taken quickly on a wet counter amid the unmistakable odor of sizzling grease. Nedick's —which sponsored, and was a part of, Marty Glickman's play-by-play broadcasts of the college doubleheaders. Marty Glickman meant basketball in New York then, his articulate rapid-fire staccato set to the beat of big-city rhythms: "Another-rebound-up-no-good, another-rebound-up-no-good, and Roman clears the boards. Here comes City on a fast break, Warner from the top of the key, swish." Or: "It's good, like Nedick's," he would shout on occasion when a shot was made. But mostly it was swish. Swish, he would cry, and you would hang on the magic of the word the way a later generation would wait breathless for Marv Albert's rasping "Yes."

Once inside the Garden, you began the slow ascent up what certainly was the steepest bank of stairs in America. There were no ramps, no elevators, no escalators, and so you climbed those stairs to the very top, to the balcony, and you looked out into an arena that would be a revelation to one who knew only its replacement. The new Garden, which sits like a theater-in-the-round on the site of Pennsylvania Station, is a sybaritic palace of pastels, cushioned seats, and soaring escalators. It is bright, airy, comfortable, and plush. There are no pillars to obstruct one's view. It offers, in fact, every balm to the body, but there is little to nourish the mood. What is missing, simply, is the airless scent of high drama, the big-city feel of lightning in the nerves and cold steel in the veins. The new Garden, one suspects, was designed to appeal to the tastes of suburban America, while the old building resembled the maw of the city in which it was built. It was a hard gray angular structure, as rugged and tough as the streets of Harlem or the back alleys of the Bronx. It was an awesome arena, almost solemn in its aspect. It had about it the air of a great cathedral, and well it might have, for the game of basketball was a native ritual in New York, and Madison Square Garden was its Mecca.

Just before the game was to start, the lights in the stands would dim and a spotlight would fall on the American flag that hung vertically from the roof above center court. The National Anthem was played by Gladys Gooding at the organ, and then the court would light up with a brightness that burned back at the eyes. The polished hardwood of the Garden floor glistened through the darkness with the refractive glare of light cast through a teardrop. In the seconds before the players came onto the floor, while they huddled at their benches, hands joined in the center, one might look down and count off the fifteen feet from base line to foul line and think what it might be like, ball in hand, to fix on the front of that rim, to look through the glass of the backboard and see the silence of the crowd. What might it be like to play a game of basketball on the court of Madison

Square Garden? Are those rims as tight and as live as they seem? Does the floor yield easily to the touch of the ball? Can you hear it now, can you really hear the sounds, the muffled drumbeat of those sneakered feet, the squeak of rubber against hardwood, can you feel the texture of the ball, that big bright globe with the pimpled surface, the black cut seams beneath the tips of your fingers? Yes, you can feel it, you can feel that familiar touch, soft as a kiss, when the ball leaves the fingertips on its lonely lover's tryst. You can feel it that way when it is right and true, almost as if the ball never leaves your hand, you can feel it and you don't have to track it with your eyes, you can just listen for it, you can listen for the soft whoosh. "Swish," says Marty Glickman, "good, like Nedick's," and your back is already turned when your name is spoken across the city to the armies of New York's own, who have dreamed the same city dream and who, in the quiet of their secret hearts, can hear your name spoken as their own.

Bradley had won fourteen games in a row going into the finals, and the Braves opened up as if they were serious about number fifteen. They sped to a 29–18 lead after fourteen minutes and now, for the first time in the tournament, City would be obliged to come from behind. The Beavers had been playing poorly. Their shooting was off, their passing was erratic, they could not hit from the foul line, they were being beaten off the boards. They found they could fast-break against Bradley, but they were missing the lay-ups. The team appeared to be unnerved. At one point, Roth blew the easy basket on a four-on-one fast break, and Holman lifted him in favor of the more experienced Norm Mager. Mager had been used sparingly during the regular season, and his insertion in the lineup seemed to be one of those moves that come to a winner by way of inspiration. The game turned almost immediately. Mager gave the team some badly needed rebounding and tightened up the defense. Bradley played the last six minutes of the half without scoring a field goal, and City scored nine straight points to close to within 30–27.

Both teams came out running in the second half, and the score was tied six times and the lead changed hands seven times during the next fifteen minutes. Roman put City ahead at 57–56, and Dambrot followed with a three-point play. Bradley was being outrun, they began to show signs of exhaustion. Melchiorre fouled out, and with Mager taking key rebounds and Warner driving repeatedly to the rim, City eased its way to a 69–61 victory and the NIT title. Dambrot led the scoring with twenty-three points, followed by Roman with nineteen, and Warner with sixteen. Warner was voted the tournament's most valuable player. It was the first time that honor had gone to a black man.

Blacks were still, in fact, called Negroes then, and rare was the mention of Warner or Layne that neglected to note their color. Their number in college basketball was exceedingly few. It had been only three years since Jackie Robinson, who was the Pacific Coast scoring leader for UCLA in 1939–40, broke into major-league baseball. There had never been an official color line in basketball, but then none was necessary. Most basketball players went to school on athletic scholarships, and not many of them were made available to black athletes. Most of those who made it went to Negro colleges such as Grambling and Winston-Salem, and a very few made it to the pro ranks. It would be almost two decades before black basketball players, who learned their game in the swift, tough playgrounds of Harlem and South Philadelphia, would be courted and recruited by the big colleges and finally, in the seventies, become the sport's dominant force at both the college and professional levels.

Warner and Layne were the only two blacks on the predominantly Jewish team that brought CCNY its first tournament championship. City had been to the NIT three times previously and had never gotten past the semifinals. In 1949 it was eliminated in the opening round. In its lone NCAA appearance, it had reached the eastern finals before losing to Holy Cross. Now, as NIT champions, the team was toasted at dinners and rallies throughout the city.

The players were received by Mayor William O'Dwyer on the steps of City Hall before hundreds of students, faculty, and the college band. Holman, who had sat through the Bradley game with a temperature of one hundred and three, was represented by Bobby Sand, the assistant coach, and Sam Winograd, the athletic director.

O'Dwyer shook the hand of each player and said, "I congratulate you for making the City of New York so proud." Noon classes were unofficially suspended for an impromptu rally attended by more than two thousand students. Dr. Harry N. Wright, president of the college, presided at the rally. "I think a great deal of this team as individuals," he said, "and I feel that its play last week typified the true spirit of CCNY." The whirlwind pace continued for two days. Some of the players were honored at dinners, others appeared on radio programs, and there were spontaneous celebrations in their neighborhoods in the Bronx, Brooklyn, and Manhattan.

On the third day the team rested. The following night it would open its quest for the NCAA title against Ohio State, the number-two-ranked team in the country, and the entire city seemed to be holding its breath. Little attention was paid to the fact that the New York Knickerbockers had beaten the Washington Capitols 103–83 and were about to take on the Syracuse Nationals in the semifinals of the NBA playoffs. Pro basketball took second billing in those days. In fact, the announcement had already come that if the Knicks defeated Syracuse and got to the championship round they would be unable to play their home games at the Garden. The circus was coming to town.

3

The NCAA was a regional tournament. Four eastern teams and four western teams competed among themselves, and the winners met for the championship in the East-West finals. The eastern semifinals were played as a Madison Square Garden doubleheader matching City and Ohio State in the opener, with fourth-ranked Holy Cross against fifth-placed North Carolina State in the nightcap.

Ohio State was a team devoted to fundamental basketball. It employed a tight zone defense, clogging the middle and thus preventing the opposing team from driving to the basket. On offense, the Buckeyes played a fast-paced, driving game, entrusting the scoring to All-American Dick Schnittker, who could shoot equally well with either hand, and rangy Bob Donham. It was a team likely to give City trouble, and the game was played in classic patterns. The two teams traded baskets for most of the first half, neither able to open a significant lead, and the score was tied 40–40 at intermission.

City took a three-point lead early in the second half, and then Holman introduced a new strategy to counter the effects of the zone. The Beavers held the ball, declining to shoot from the outside or work the ball toward the basket. The intent was to force Ohio State to come after the ball, to draw the defense out and open the middle to new lanes of attack. But Ohio State did not take the bait. It waited patiently, and for almost five minutes nothing at all happened. Then City started to shoot over the zone, and the pace of the game accelerated. Floyd Layne and Norm Mager, neither known for the accuracy of their long-range shooting, each hit seven times from the outside. But still, Ohio State stayed close and played cool even when City tried to freeze away a two-point lead.

The Beavers elected to take advantage of the experimental two-minute book rule, long since abandoned, which permitted a team that was fouled in the final two minutes of a game to keep possession of the ball after shooting its free throw, regardless of whether the shot was made or missed. The effect of the rule was that the team that was trailing could not get the ball unless the other team was pressed into committing an error. That is what happened. With one minute remaining, Dambrot found Warner all alone under the basket. Warner could have taken the easy lay-up for a four-point lead, or he could have brought the ball back outside and continued the freeze. Apparently confused, he held the ball in the foul lane for more than three seconds, a violation of the rules, and the ball was turned over to Ohio State. But the Buckeyes were unable to capitalize on the opportunity, and the clock wound into the final twenty seconds with City in possession of the ball and the lead. Then the team stumbled into yet another error of judgment that almost cost it the game. Roman, driving for the basket, was called for charging into Bob Burkholder. Burkholder converted the free throw to make the score 56–55, and Ohio State had the ball out of bounds with a chance at the game-winning basket. Schnittker and Donham had fouled out earlier, and the ball went to Jim Remington in the forecourt. Remington could not work free, finally tossing up a shot with five seconds left. Roth came down with the rebound and held it till the final buzzer.

In the second game, North Carolina State's high-powered scoring machine ran away from Holy Cross 87–74. Sam Ranzino set an NCAA scoring record for State with thirty-two points, and right behind him was his teammate Dick Dickey with twenty-five. North

Carolina State was an entirely different team from Ohio State. It played with a wide-open, almost reckless frenzy, and Ranzino and Dickey threatened to turn any game into a shooting gallery. Curiously, though, City's meeting with Carolina followed much the same script as its contest with Ohio State.

Again the game went down to the last two minutes, with City nursing a three-point lead after the score had been tied fourteen times. And again the Beavers succeeded in fouling out the opposition's two big guns, Ranzino and Dickey, in the closing minutes. Roman, too, had been forced to leave the game on fouls, but City had the proper counter. Warner went into the pivot and feinted his way to a pair of lay-ups, one with the left hand and one with the right, to give the Beavers a five-point closing margin, 78–73.

And so it came down to the finals, and once more the opponent would be Bradley. Ironically, Bradley was the last team to gain an NCAA berth. It had been deadlocked with Kansas in District Five, and a playoff game was postponed to allow Bradley to compete in the NIT. Thus, the day after its grueling loss to CCNY, Bradley flew to Kansas City for a second chance against a strong Kansas team led by six-foot-nine Clyde Lovellette. It was a rugged game for the Braves, not decided until the last three minutes when Paul Unruh scored three field goals in forty-five seconds to earn a 59–57 decision and a place in the western regionals of the NCAA. Bradley appeared to be a tired team, beating UCLA after trailing late in the second half and then barely edging past a Baylor team that was a fourteen-point underdog. The next day, the team made the trip to New York for its Tuesday-night rematch with CCNY.

City would be trying to accomplish a feat that was without precedent. Four times in the past ten years teams had tried for a grand slam of both the NIT and NCAA, and none had ever gotten this close. Colorado won the NIT title in 1939–40, but was beaten by Southern California in the western semifinals of the NCAA. That same season, Duquesne lost to Colorado in the NIT championship game and then lost to Indiana in the eastern finals. In 1943–44, Utah won the NCAA championship after losing to Kentucky in the quarterfinals of the NIT, and Kentucky, favored to sweep both tourneys in 1948–49, never made it past the opening round of the NIT.

Now City would have its chance, and the sentiment all over town was that the Beavers, outmatched or not, would find a way to win it. Even the usually cautious Holman seemed to exude a rare confidence. "The team," he said, "just seemed to arrive in the Kentucky game during the Invitation. I don't think they have been lucky and I don't think they've been just hot. They simply found themselves."

But the feeling in New York, on the street corners and in the schoolyards and pool halls, was not so much one of confidence as one of faith. It was as if the New Yorkers had locked hands with destiny. Yes, destiny was the shield that would turn even their frailties to strength. Bradley had only its basketball skills to govern its fortunes; City could dip into deeper realms; it could, if needed, call forth the magic of the charnel house.

Indeed, the uninitiated at the Garden on the night of the game might have thought they had ventured into a primitive den of black magic and voodoo. Long before the start of the game, the Garden vibrated to the sound of "Allagaroo." "Allagaroo," the City College war cry, was likely a corruption of the French *à la guerre*, meaning "on to the war," but beyond that little thought was paid to its derivation. It was the droning pitch that lent the aura: "Allagaroo, garoo, garah; Allagaroo, garoo, garah; Ee-yah, Ee-yah, Sis, Boom, Bah." It was less a cheer than an incantation that might yet raise a demon or two, for it suggested the promise of some mysterious alliance with dark forces. And as the Beavers prepared to take the floor against Bradley, you could hear it rise up, slowly, as if from some bottomless depth, and then roll out in waves, out and up, and then cascade back upon itself, only to start up again when the players joined hands at their bench and then broke and eddied out onto the floor.

Basketball is the only team sport in which the players do not trot out onto the playing surface at the start of a game. They leave their huddle and ease out slowly, tentatively, perhaps to husband their energy for nonstop play, perhaps because they feel their opponent must be stalked before he is met. It is a small eternity for a basketball player, those few slow moments before he takes his place on the court, touches hands with the man he is playing against, and waits for the tip-off. It is a time to contemplate the possibilities of victory and defeat, to know that in the space of forty minutes on the playing clock he will again live a lifetime, and that his brief epitaph will be written, for all to see, in the electric numbers on the scoreboard.

Jumping center for City was Ed Roman from Taft High School in the Bronx. Roman, six foot six and 220 pounds, slightly stooped at the shoulders, had an easy gait and a broad, rounded face that seemed always about to open into a grin. His unorthodox shape had earned him the nickname Goose early in the season, but he didn't like the name, and it soon faded from use. Roman had never played basketball until Marty Force, the Taft coach, spotted him in his sophomore year. Then he sat on the bench and watched Irwin Dambrot set new scoring records. The following season, Dambrot broke his wrist, and Roman broke his scoring record with 360 points. It did not come without effort. Roman spent nine hours a day at practice. He was serious about the game, but he took his success lightly. The day after City won the NIT title, Roman was playing three-man ball in the Claremont Park schoolyard. He had scored more points in a single season than any City player before him, he was the team's leading rebounder, and though he was not noted for his defensive play, no one would soon forget the job he did on Bill Spivey and Dick Schnittker in the tournaments.

Ed Warner and Irwin Dambrot opened at the forwards. Warner, from De Witt Clinton High School in the Bronx, had closed the season as the team's principal threat. There was nothing he could not do on a basketball court. He could shoot from outside or in close, he could rebound, he constituted a fast break all by himself. Holman had called him the toughest pivot man in the game, and there were few to give argument. Warner first picked up a basketball on Lenox Avenue in Harlem when he was ten years old and he never let it go. He went from the church team at St. Philip's to the big team at the Harlem Y, and led both Frederick Douglass Junior High School and

De Witt Clinton to city championships. He had a magnificent build for an athlete—lean and muscular with hands that wrapped around a basketball as if it were an orange. Warner was intent, almost somber in his mood. He rarely smiled. He had grown up tough in Harlem, and he knew that life was serious business. And basketball was a large part of his life.

Dambrot was the only senior on the starting five. He was a solid, complete ball player, the classic forward, and a coach's dream. Early in the season, Holman had called him "the greatest player I ever coached." He was an All-American type—bright, personable, even-tempered, moving steadily and surely toward a career as a dentist. He had been married after his junior year, and he and his wife lived with his parents in a three-room walk-up in the Bronx. His wife would help put him through dental school. On the court, he was consistent rather than electrifying. He was a strong rebounder, a playmaker, a steadying influence on a fundamentally sophomore team. Dambrot averaged ten points a game during the regular season, and he was never the team's high scorer. But in the NIT final, he led all scorers with twenty-three points and held Bradley's All-American, Paul Unruh, to fifteen. Now he would match up with Unruh again.

In the backcourt were Floyd Layne and Al Roth. Layne, from Benjamin Franklin High School in Manhattan, was about as tall as Warner but some thirty pounds lighter. He was sleek and wiry and racehorse swift, and he possessed an uncanny instinct for the ball. He seemed to be always in motion, his long arms churning in windmill fashion, slapping the ball loose, his hand thrust in the face of his opponent. Layne was the team's best defensive player, and he was continually spoken of as underrated. "Hell," Layne said, "that's a compliment. When they start calling you underrated, they've already started overrating you." It was a typical reaction. Layne was easygoing, quick-witted, articulate, and modest. He had started his high school career at Clinton, but he felt he was not good enough for the team. "If you make the team at Clinton," he said, "you're some-body." He transferred to Franklin, where he was coached by Bill Spiegel, and where the only white player on the team was Zeke

Sinicola, who later starred for Niagara. Curiously, basketball was not his best sport. He was a left-handed pitcher on City's baseball team, and he harbored visions of pitching in the major leagues.

Roth, who led Brooklyn's Erasmus Hall to a city title, had received scholarship offers from colleges like Duke, George Washington, and Duquesne, but he chose City because he wanted to stay at home. Roth was a stocky little playmaker who had peeled off more than twenty pounds during the course of the season, but was still known as Fats or Tubby. He had learned to play basketball in the PS 161 schoolyard in the Crown Heights section of Brooklyn, across the street from his home. He had started young, and by the time he was sixteen, he said, "I was eating, drinking, and dreaming basketball." Roth was the team's feeder, the assist man, but he was an uneven shooter and too small to rebound. During the tournaments, much of his playing time was going to Norm Mager, a senior.

Mager, called the Splinter, was six foot two and 133 pounds when he played for Lafayette High School in Brooklyn. He had attended St. John's briefly, and then, during World War II, he served two and a half years in the Air Force. When the war ended, he enrolled at City because he would have had to wait six months before returning to St. John's. He had grown three inches now and put on fifty-five pounds, but his mother still insisted he was too thin to play basketball. Mager had appeared in all of City's games, but he had seen little playing time. He averaged only a shade better than three points a game during the season, but he had scored fifteen against Ohio State and nine against North Carolina State in the NCAA, and he would play a major role in the championship game against Bradley.

So it was those six—Roman, Warner, Dambrot, Layne, Roth, and Mager—who carried City's fortunes into the last game of the season. They were not, to the eye of the youthful observer, an awesome-looking unit. They were, after all, not much past their teens. Roman, in fact, was just nineteen. Warner, Layne, and Roth were twenty, Dambrot a year older, and Mager was twenty-four. For that reason alone, a high school junior would have little difficulty identifying with them. There were other reasons.

Basketball players invariably appear to be more human, which is to say less legendary as figures, than athletes in other sports. They are not, for one thing, cloaked in uniforms that inspire awe. There is no true basketball equivalent of Yankee pinstripes or the black and orange of the Chicago Bears. A basketball uniform exposes the man so that he is, finally, comprehensible. The numbers on the back are superfluous. One can identify the players, even from a seat in the balcony, by the cut of their features, the style of their hair, by the countless unnamed mannerisms by which we recognize an acquaintance half a block away.

And the nature of the sport itself contributes to the sense of intimacy. A teen-ager, even one who was an exceptional baseball player, could not possibly identify with Joe DiMaggio. He might admire his genius, even idolize the imposing grace of his presence, he could pattern himself after DiMaggio, assume his stance at bat, attempt to emulate his every movement, but he would know that even on his best day he could not presume to hit a Bobby Feller fastball. But basketball is different; it is the most personal of team sports. Reduced to its essentials, it is a game in which a player is required to shoot a ball through a hoop ten feet above the ground, and the refinements of that act require no cooperation. You can watch a player miss an easy shot or blow a pair from the foul line and feel, with absolute certainty, that you could have made those shots. A long set shot, true to target, is fundamentally no different in a playground from what it is in Madison Square Garden, and a good schoolyard player can, on occasion, compare himself favorably with the best basketball player in the country.

So that was part of it, a large part of it, but there was an element that cut even deeper, which was that you could feel a particular kinship with these people because you shared not only their aspirations but their roots. You came from the same streets and went to the same schools and you both knew the good sweet taste of a Mission orange drunk from the bottle at the corner candy store. You could not know for sure, but you suspected that they did not drink Mission orange in Peoria, Illinois, which is where Bradley was located. Where was Peoria, Illinois, anyway? It was out there somewhere, way west of New Jersey, in another country, where they never heard of an egg cream and didn't have a subway to ride or any major-league baseball teams, and they probably didn't play stickball in the streets and measure the length of their hits by the distance between sewers. Peoria was small-town America, with its backyards and Main Streets, its high school pep rallies on Friday nights, a town crammed with filling stations where you took the girl next door to the bowling alley or to the ice-cream parlor after a neighborhood movie. It was not a real city out there, you knew that for sure. They didn't have the dark tough streets to contend with or the hot nights spent sitting on stoops or riding the upper deck of a Fifth Avenue bus. They didn't have to invent games that could be played in tight quarters with nothing more than a pink Spaldeen, with the edge of a tenement for the foul pole and the fenders of cars serving as bases. Probably they had learned to shoot baskets at rims fixed above the garage door. It was a different America out there; they likely had voted twice for Tom Dewey.

And for certain they did not have a City College in Peoria, a college that was open to every resident of the city who could qualify, where one could get a four-year education without its costing a dime, where one's own father, who ten years earlier did not have a word of English on his tongue, could gain admission without a dollar in his pocket. City College was something special in New York. We had no need here of Harvard or Yale, for we had a school that had produced its full share of Supreme Court Justices and scientists and writers, and they were all our own, they were our neighbors, and we had paid for their education with our tax money. So long as there was a City College every kid in New York knew that he had a chance. It did not matter whether his father had gone there before him, or where his ancestors came from, or how much money he could muster. There were no quotas and no restrictions and no phony scholarships. If you were a New Yorker and could pass the test, City College would be glad to have you. You could not believe they had a college like that in Peoria because, it seemed to you, only New York understood that kind of thing, only New York chose to offer free education to sons of immigrants and grandsons of slaves.

Who is to say how much of that was involved in this last game with Bradley? Who is to say that one did not intimate here the symbolic collision of two Americas? Who would say finally that there was not the faintest suggestion of reverse bigotry at work and that one was not entirely guiltless? For, after all, look down there on the court and let your heart shape the words to describe it: Yes, five street kids from the City of New York—three Jews and two blacks—were about to whale the shit out of middle America.

4

Bradley had played City man-to-man the last time they met, but now they changed tactics and used a zone defense in an effort to neutralize City's speed. Zone defenses come in an almost infinite variety, but they are all designed toward one end: to prevent a team from driving to the basket, thus forcing it to take long-range shots, to shoot over the zone. The conventional basketball defense pits one man against another, creating, in effect, five individual contests within a single game. The zone is a team defense. In its most standard form, the three big men—the center and two forwards—protect sections, or zones, around the basket. The two guards act as chasers, always moving with the flow of the ball. Therefore, should an offensive player drive past the first line of defense, he will be met immediately by other defenders as he moves into a new zone. Ideally, then, the man with the ball always attracts multiple defenders, the lanes leading to the basket are congested, and the offensive team is obliged to shoot from a distance.

The best way to break a zone is to fast-break on it, to rush the ball into the forecourt before the defensive team has a chance to set itself up. But this can be done only with the rebound of a missed shot, for if the shot is made the zone-playing team will always have sufficient time to fall back and establish its defense. Once the defense is set, a team's options are limited. Dribbling against the zone is anathema. The attacking team must pass the ball swiftly and accurately, making the defense work hard, keeping it in constant motion. Since the players cannot move as quickly as the ball is passed, a man will be left open for an outside shot. If those shots are made with some consistency, the zone will lose its intended effect.

That is the strategy with which City countered. Roman, playing outside to spread the zone wide, scored twelve points in the first twelve minutes on six outside shots, and City moved to an early lead and held it through the first half, finishing with a 39–32 advantage. In the second half, Bradley abandoned its zone in favor of a man-to-man defense. The Beavers then turned to their running game and continued to stretch their lead, increasing the margin to ten midway through the second half.

But Bradley now had gone to a full-court press, and the constant pressure was taking its toll on City. The team appeared to grow weary, its passes lost their snap and precision, and then, with nine minutes left in the game, Roman fouled out. The steady din under which the game had been played stilled now as Bradley began to cut methodically into the lead. It was down to five with two minutes to go, and then Melchiorre stole a pass and dribbled half the length of the court, and the score stood at 66–63. Then the din turned to bedlam as City answered back. Mager converted a free throw, and Dambrot took a perfect pass from Layne to give City a six-point edge with only fifty-seven seconds remaining, and the game appeared to be under lock. But with the suddenness of a flare struck in darkness, Bradley was back at the door. Joe Stowell made a foul shot, and then Melchiorre, with hands as quick as a card shark's, went into his act. He picked up a stray ball and drove in for a lay-up, and less than twenty seconds later he performed an encore, intercepting a City pass and again going the length of the court to make the score 69–68. Now City took the ball out beneath its own basket with a one-point lead that required protection for some forty seconds. Bradley pressed tight in the backcourt, and again Melchiorre picked off a wild pass and drove for home. This time he found the path to the basket guarded, and he pulled up at the foul line for a short jump shot that would put his team ahead. But he had the much taller Dambrot to contend with. Dambrot reached up, blocked the shot, and somehow managed to retain control of the ball. Then, like a quick-armed quarterback, he fired the length of the court to a sprinting Norm Mager, the other senior on the court, who laid the ball in the basket with less than ten seconds showing on the clock. The score was 71–68. The game was over.

The beautiful balance of the City team was reflected in the scoring totals. Dambrot, voted the game's outstanding player, led City with fifteen points. Mager, who had five stitches taken in his forehead after a first-half collision with Aaron Preece, returned to score fourteen, a total matched by Warner. Roman had no more than the twelve with which he opened the game, and Layne finished with eleven. The remaining five points were made by Al Roth. Melchiorre was the game's top scorer with sixteen points, and Unruh, outplayed for the second straight time by Dambrot, was held to eight.

That night, Irving Spiegel wrote in the *Times*, "It was 'Allagaroo' through the canyons, the side streets, on Times Square, Fifth Avenue, and all over the Borough of Manhattan, through the night and late into the afternoon."

At eleven-thirty on the morning after the game, some two thousand students left City's School of Business at Twenty-third Street and Lexington Avenue and walked to the main campus in West Harlem. There, classes were suspended at noon, and more than six thousand students swarmed across the center mall, many climbing trees to gain a better vantage point for the biggest rally the school had ever seen. The roars for the players seemed to swell from the ground, rising in a vibrating crescendo and bouncing in echoes from the walls of the Gothic structures that dotted the campus. The tower bell atop the Main Building pealed for five minutes.

President Harry N. Wright, making his second campus speech within ten days, told the students, "This is one of the proudest days of my life. This team came here to study, not to play basketball. I am proud of the team and what it has done for the college. I want to point out that they are given no scholarships to play ball, and they have not been imported to play basketball. I am particularly proud of their high scholastic rating."

Norm Mager missed the speech. He had been taking a midterm examination, and when he came by for a last-minute appearance he was treated to a thunderous ovation. The round of honors continued for more than a week. On April 6 the entire team was honored by Borough President Robert F. Wagner. The players were presented with engraved scrolls, and Nat Holman was sworn in as Honorary Deputy Commissioner of the Borough of Manhattan. To make the new position a legal office, Holman was paid the fee of six cents before he took his oath.

At the same ceremony, held in Dr. Wright's office, the president announced that City would turn down an invitation to represent the United States in the first Pan-American Olympic Games to be held the following year in Argentina. The Games, Dr. Wright pointed out, would be played during February and March, while school was in session, and the players could not be excused from classes.

Four days later, a group of former City College players declined another invitation, this one less noted but perhaps of greater significance. Three seniors and four alumni who had been scheduled to appear in an exhibition game May 1 in St. Nicholas Arena, withdrew from the game when they learned it would be part of a May Day program, sponsored by the *Daily Worker*, the newspaper of the American Communist Party. The players—seniors Mike Wittlin, Joe Galiber, and Leroy Watkins, and alumni Hilty Shapiro, Sonny Jameson, Lionel Malamed, and Phil Farbman—were to play professionally against another pickup team. They said they had not been aware of Communist Party involvement, and withdrew immediately upon being notified.

There was yet another piece of basketball news that season. On April 19, Paul Unruh reported that he had been offered a bribe during the National Invitation Tournament. Unruh said he had been approached by an unidentified man in front of his Manhattan hotel and asked if he would like to "make some easy money." The man offered Unruh one hundred dollars if Bradley won any tournament game by under seven points, and five hundred dollars if the margin was held under three. Unruh said he brushed the man off and went on his way. He did not report it because he thought it was unimportant. No one else thought it was important either. The announcement was given four inches on page 41 of *The New York Times,* and nobody paid much attention.

Yet it is just such events—a bribe lightly offered and casually declined, a game of basketball canceled because of its political implications—that sometimes give suggestion to larger events. The color of an entire decade might have been found there, the first intimations of a festering dread that would skin the soul from the country through all the years of the fifties. Indeed, it had already begun.

The season just past had linked the moods of two very different decades in America. We had long been a nation whose warring impulses did battle at the borders of schizophrenia, not quite able to distinguish between the reality outside us and the imperatives of the imagination. And that is a difficulty which was buried deep in our roots. We were capable at the same time of the most profound largesse and the pettiest of recriminations. We could declare at once our devotion to liberty and proceed to protect it with the most ferocious fevers of repression. We were able, in the forties, to summon the fine dimensions of a selfless valor, and then, a decade later, our dreams could be turned to ashes by the specter of an imagined foe.

Yes, it had already begun. Before the season was half over, 202 employees of the State Department had been dismissed as security risks. On the day that City beat Southern Methodist for its third win of the season, the House Committee on Un-American Activities was investigating a former Vice-President, Henry Wallace, and a former adviser to a President, Harry L. Hopkins, as having been instrumental in funneling atomic secrets to the Soviet Union. A day later, on December 9, Chiang Kai-shek's Chinese Nationalists moved their capital to Formosa, and after nearly three decades of civil war, China had been won by Mao's Communists. One cannot begin to overestimate the importance of that event, for it lit the light of madness in America.

If one can assume that nations are governed by psychic forces no less profound than those that reside in the individual, they are doubtless prey to the same disorders. And the first stirrings of madness begin at that precise moment when one finds he can no longer contain the contradictions that boil within him. We were a land of free men that was built by slaves; a nation of revolutionaries that feared nothing so much as revolution; a country whose best capitalistic instincts told it that all ideas would have their chance in the open market, but now, having garnered our treasures, it was equally devoted to the restraint of trade.

The momentum was building. In the late forties, the Congress and the states had passed into law a slew of security acts (virtually all of which, years later, would be ruled unconstitutional), and now, early in the fifties, the courts were busy upholding them. On February 10, a federal court declared it was constitutional to deport an alien for past membership in a subversive organization. On March 8, New York State's Feinberg Law, requiring all public school teachers to take an oath of loyalty to the federal government, was upheld as valid. Two weeks later, the U.S. Court of Appeals ruled that the government had the right to dismiss, arbitrarily and without benefit of rebuttal, any employee regarded as a security risk. These were not laws intended as symbolic gestures. They were being put to quick use. On the day before the NIT final, the government of the United States was preparing to try no fewer than twelve thousand persons under the Smith Act.

That was the smallest part of it. Laws, no matter how repressive, must at least be ground through the machinery of the courts. The accused would have his say. But now something new was afoot. Investigations were under way. The House had been busy for some time, and now the Senate was at work. Its Foreign Relations Subcommittee, on March 9, began an official search for Communists in the State Department. There was at least one senator who gave reason to believe that investigations were unnecessary, and certainly lacking in dramatic content. Joseph R. McCarthy had come to the center of America's stage with as much flair and as little grace as an overweight stripper in a small-town gin mill. Once the first glove dropped, there was none to tell just where it might end. And he went into his act as though buoyed by the knowledge that he and the cops shared the same employer. Hardly a day passed without new names and numbers being dropped as if at auction. It was Dorothy Kenyon and Ambassador Philip C. Jessup; Haldore E. Hanson of the Point Four Program on one day and John Stewart Service summoned home from India the next. Finally, as the month of March waned, McCarthy, with much fanfare and not the first offer of evidence, would name Professor Owen Lattimore, a State Department adviser for Far Eastern affairs, as the "top Russian espionage agent" in the United States.

Certainly, that would be the focus. It would come down to the Far East, to China, a civilization thousands of years older than our own that somehow, through fits of the most tortured thought, we had come to believe was the rightful property of the United States. How else to explain the recurrent charge from the right that the Truman administration had "lost" China. Lost it!—as though it were the stake in a crap game, destined to exchange hands on the roll of the dice. Yes indeed, this was just the beginning. The China Lobby was now counting its numbers, McCarthy was taking careful inventory. And the worst was yet to come. Three months later, in June, we would be at war in Korea.

But this was still early spring. One must assume that Far Eastern affairs and congressional investigations were remote from the minds of the City College grand-slam team as the players accepted their honors with all proper grace. Equally remote, in all probability, were the implications of the unheeded news items that seven players had withdrawn from a May Day basketball game and that a bribe had been offered during the NIT. They were simply the first suggestions that a great cloud, filled with the fiercest fury and the deepest midnight darkness, lay brooding somewhere on the horizon. Both the nation and its only true native sport would soon know some of their bleakest hours. The game of basketball, and its reigning champions, would suffer the swiftest blow.

PART
TWO

5

Basketball has always been a paradox of a sport. It is the most elegant, the most gracefully aesthetic of all games, and yet it is stark in its simplicity. It is a game played man against man, but each direct confrontation finally swirls into the most intricate patterns of cooperation, swoops and leaps that offer the high drama of theater and the blessings of improvised ballet. It is a polite competition, a courtly game, in which a player is subject to penalty if he so much as touches his opponent, but only boxing requires a greater discipline of the body. Basketball is that most American of sports, both regal and corrupt; a pagan rite manipulated by scoundrels and sanctified by saints.

Of course, it is a game that grew up during the Depression in the dungeons of big cities, and it has always held attraction for the underworld. As long ago as 1931, the *Brooklyn Eagle* reported that Max Posnack, captain of the St. John's Wonder Five, had been offered three thousand dollars to throw a game with Manhattan College. Three thousand dollars was a princely sum to turn down in 1931, when it is considered that twenty years later substantially smaller fees were found to be adequate. But the size of the offer is unimportant. It was still early, 1931, the very first year that college basketball left its own precincts. The fair market price had not yet been established.

Two decades later, Jimmy Cannon, the sports writer, would call basketball "the slot machine of sports." It was a fair enough metaphor, for both can be rigged to satisfaction with just the slightest bit of tampering. A basketball game is often won or lost on nuances so subtle they are lost to the practiced eye. Even the slightest break in the rhythm of a game—a half second lost on a fast break, an extra dribble before passing or shooting, a defensive position that leaves a driving lane open—can cost a basket or give one away. More than a small degree of skill is required to dump a basketball game without its being detected.

Forddy Anderson, the coach of Bradley, viewed the films of a fixed game and felt free to admit: "I've studied the movies of the Oregon State game at least twenty times and can't find a single play which indicates the kids weren't giving their best efforts every second."

The definitive critique, though, was given by an unidentified player who had learned the skill well. "When the point spread is big enough —say, eight to twelve points—a small group of players can control the points without the slightest danger of being detected by their coach or even their own teammates. As a matter of fact, a couple of really smart operators can win a game for their team—grab off the headlines as the stars of the game—and still make the score come out the way the gamblers want it!"

The key, of course, is the point spread, the margin by which one team is expected to beat the other. It was the advent of the "spread," or the "price," or the "line," in the early forties that finally wed basketball to the big gambling interests. Until then, a bettor would simply get odds on a game, as is still the custom in sports like baseball or boxing. If a team was an eight-to-five favorite, on a straight betting basis, a bettor would put up eight dollars to win five if he wanted the favorite, or five to win eight if he chose the underdog. But the action on basketball was slow. It is an axiom of gambling that betting odds are sweets for the sucker. It does not matter how good the odds are if your team loses. Conversely, if one wishes to put his money on a heavy favorite, say six-to-one, he finds he must make a substantial investment on the chance of winning a rather small sum. As a consequence, very few bettors were prepared to risk their money on a game between two mismatched teams. And so the bookmakers, ever resourceful, devised the point spread.

The first point spreads covered a three-point range. A team, for example, might be quoted as a six-eight favorite, which meant that the favorite would have to win by eight points or more for the bettor to collect, while a bet on the underdog would be good if it lost the game by six or fewer. It was the middle point that was the killer, for if the favorite won by seven points, all bets were lost. The bettors were quick to discover the hazards of the system. An unusually large number of games seemed to hit the middle. Nobody won. And so an adjustment was made. Only one point line was given, usually with a half point tacked on to avert a tie or, in gambler's parlance, a "push." Thus if a team was a seven-and-a-half-point favorite it would have to win by eight for its backers to collect. If it won by seven or fewer, it was a payday for the underdog. With the point spread invoked, all games were, theoretically, even propositions. The spread was the great equalizer.

Basketball soon became the most heavily bet sport in America. The spread was the gambler's delight and every balm to the bookmaker. It made every game a toss-up. It also made it possible for a team to win a game on the board and still lose it to the points. New possibilities were opened up. A gambler wishing to insure a big bet might offer a piece of the profits to a player or two on the favored team. All they would have to do was to stay under the spread. They would not, after all, be dumping the game. What difference did it make whether the team won by seven or five? The player would be able to win twice—he could win both the game and the bet—not by dumping, but by shaving the points. One could make his pact with the devil and still remain on the side of the angels. Wasn't that the Great American Dream?

It is not possible to estimate how many times that covenant was closed. No reliable record is kept of bribe offers, whether accepted or aborted, but it would not be imprudent to assume that for every one that comes to public attention there might be ten (and who would not say fifty) that remain the private business of the parties involved.

Vadal Peterson, the coach of the University of Utah, did not, for instance, report an offer made to him in New York in March 1944 on the eve of his team's NCAA championship game with Dartmouth in Madison Square Garden. The revelation came seven months later by way of Phog Allen, the University of Kansas coach, who said that a gambler had come to Peterson's hotel room and asked him how much it would cost to have Utah lose the game. Peterson is said to have answered the question, in the best Hollywood tradition, with a right cross. The following night, by way of affirmation, his team went out to defeat Dartmouth 42–40.

It was a minor incident, never directly reported, never really a part of the public record; more an anecdote, a small slice of Americana than an instance of attempted bribery. Peterson simply had done what any red-blooded college coach would have done under the circumstances. For it was, after all, 1944, a time when all of our heroes were cut to mythological dimensions. The grim shroud of the thirties was being lifted to the dawn. We had, somehow, managed to survive the storm winds whistling down the tunnels of our darkest night, and who among us then would be the first to doubt the silent strength that beat in the great good heart of America?

So a year passed before there appeared the first real chink in the armor. On January 30, 1945, five Brooklyn College players admitted they had accepted bribes to lose a game to Akron College in Boston Garden. They also confessed they were planning to throw a Madison Square Garden game that night against St. Francis of Brooklyn. The St. Francis game was canceled. The players identified the men who engineered the bribe as Harry Rosen and Harvey Stemmer, both of Brooklyn. The pair was convicted on May 10, three days after the war in Europe ended, and each was sentenced to a year in jail and fined five hundred dollars. Stemmer was not easily reformed. A year later, he was involved in an attempt to bribe Frank Filchock and Merle

Hapes of the New York Giants to throw the National Football League championship game to the Chicago Bears. Four of the five Brooklyn players—Bob Leder, Bernard Barnett, Jerry Green, and Stanley Simon—were expelled from college. The fifth, Larry Pearlstein, was not expelled because, it was discovered later, he had never been registered as a student.

There were other scattered reports over the next few years, all of vague offers and firm refusals, but the only one of substance occurred in professional basketball. On December 10, 1948, Joe Fulks, of the Philadelphia Warriors, swore out a warrant against a small-time poolroom operator, Morris (Moxie) Fleishman, who Fulks said had made him an offer of some easy money. Fleishman was indicted on a charge of attempted bribery, but was acquitted two months later because the state had failed to prove that the "easy money" was in fact offered as payment for throwing games.

But the alarm had been sounded. If players from Brooklyn College had contracted with professional gamblers to throw two basketball games, who was ready to believe that they had been the only ones approached? If no other reports were forthcoming, that would be reassuring only to the police and the district attorney's office. The logic of the streets was woven in more intricate patterns. Each day, each season that passed without word of scandal was further evidence that games were being successfully fixed. The reasoning was sound enough.

It was not likely that Brooklyn would be the first team to suggest itself to a professional gambler looking to solidify a bet. There were stronger teams in New York. St. John's had won the NIT in 1944, and NYU went to the finals a year later. LIU and City were both nationally ranked. The action on their games would be many times the amount of money wagered on or against Brooklyn College. An unusually large bet would not be so quickly detected. No, it was not at all likely that a game between Brooklyn College and Akron, to be played in Boston halfway through the season, would be the first occasion on which thoughts of bribery would come to the minds of two New York gamblers. Yet, where was the news of previous attempts? Had they all been declined but not reported? And what could be said of subsequent seasons? Stemmer, certainly, had not entered retirement. College officials could rest easy if they chose, for not many of them were necessarily tuned to the dialect of the city.

The truth of the streets was spoken in whispers. It was a private, sometimes wordless language that was learned early and quickly and at one's own expense. The root of its syntax was that reality was too simple and subtle a thing to be trusted to language, and its style was governed by the conviction that truth required no documentation more certain than the hint of a smile or a shake of the head. The rules of evidence were the property of the courtroom, but the poolroom left nothing to chance. What was known was known by inference. No votes were taken.

And all through the postwar years of the forties, every kid in the streets of New York knew that the scores of college basketball games were being manipulated. Not all of the games, of course, not even most of them. A team would have to establish a pattern of excellence before the point spread would go high enough to warrant a fix. It was easier to convince a player to shave points, to stay under the spread, than it was to bribe him to lose a game outright. Besides, one could not go into the tank too often and still hope to escape detection. The occasional bad game would be overlooked, particularly if the team won anyway, and the gambler would have his payday. He did not mind losing now and then on the straight. A professional gambler was more than a match for the best mathematical mind when it came to percentages. He lived for the day when he could get three-to-one odds on what he knew was a legitimate two-to-one bet, and he understood the arithmetic of losing a few in order to win big.

So no elaborate explanations were required when you looked to place a bet on a college basketball game and were told no, the game was off the boards, no bets were being taken. It could mean only one of two things. Either a key player was not ready to play that game or the points had been guaranteed. If both teams showed up intact, you knew to bet the underdog. But there would be no one to take your bet.

For four years after the Brooklyn incident there was not a breath of scandal in college basketball. Then, on January 4, 1949, New York District Attorney Frank S. Hogan announced the arrest of four men for attempting to bribe David Shapiro, co-captain of George Washington University's basketball team, to fix the score of a game with Manhattan College that night in Madison Square Garden. Shapiro had been offered one thousand dollars to make certain that George Washington lost the game by more than the seven and a half points by which Manhattan was favored. Shapiro, who was twenty-five years old, a decorated veteran of World War II, and a law student at George Washington, in Washington, D.C., might not have seemed the first candidate ready to accept such an offer. He was attending school on the GI Bill, and with his veteran's benefits it was not likely he was entirely without funds. Add to that the fact that he was studying law and thus not far from the beginning of a professional career, and the conclusion might be reached that he was being asked to risk a great deal for a rather insubstantial sum of money.

Nonetheless, he was contacted at his Brooklyn home during the summer of 1948 by a man named Joseph Aronowitz, who told Shapiro there was something he wanted to discuss with him. They had their first of several meetings that day in front of the Fox Theatre in Brooklyn. There, Aronowitz told him how he could make some money during the course of the basketball season. Shapiro returned home and called the district attorney's office. Hogan, in turn, contacted Cloyd Heck Marvin, president of George Washington, and dispatched Alfred J. Scotti, chief of the Rackets Bureau, to the capital. Shapiro agreed to play bait and there transpired six months of cat-and-mouse intrigue that could have supplied the ingredients for a season's television series.

Shapiro next met with Aronowitz and two other men—Philip Klein and Jack Levy—on November 23, just before the opening of the season, at the Roger Smith Hotel in Washington. The meeting was watched by two men from the DA's office. Shapiro said he was offered one thousand dollars to "drop" a game against the University of North Carolina. Acting on instructions, he appeared noncommittal, he stalled. Some weeks later, the three men paid him an un-scheduled visit at Varsity House, on the college campus, and made him a similar offer to throw a game with the University of Virginia. Again Shapiro balked. He displayed mild interest, said he would let them know, and never called.

Then, during the Christmas holidays, Aronowitz phoned him in Brooklyn. He said they were getting impatient and that Shapiro would have to decide soon. He brought up the Manhattan game, and another meeting was arranged. They met on New Year's Eve at Penn Station, and then crossed over to the old Pennsylvania Hotel for further discussions. Now Shapiro said he was ready to make the deal but that he would need a cash advance. Shortly before noon, on the day of the game, he met Aronowitz and Klein in front of the Astor Theatre on Broadway. Shapiro was told he would be given five hundred dollars for himself and another five hundred to be distributed among his teammates to guarantee that Manhattan covered the points. Shapiro insisted on the advance, and it was agreed that the money would be paid to his uncle at seven-fifteen on the night of the game at a bar and grill on Forty-ninth Street and Eighth Avenue, opposite Madison Square Garden. The appointment was kept, and the money, stuffed in an envelope, was passed to Max Rumack, of the DA's staff, playing the part of Shapiro's uncle. Aronowitz and Klein were arrested on the spot. Levy and a fourth man, William Rivlin, were picked up later at the Airlines Terminal Building at East Forty-second Street. They were purchasing tickets to Miami. Levy, who was identified as the money man, had $4,370 in his possession. Rivlin had $900.

Shapiro, who was shaken by the events, played only a few scoreless minutes against Manhattan. He watched most of the game from the bench as his team scored a 71–65 upset victory. No one of course, and certainly not Shapiro, would find cause to wonder whether Manhattan might have been dumping for an entirely different set of gamblers. Shapiro remained in the Garden to watch City defeat St. John's in overtime in the second game of the doubleheader. Then he went to the district attorney's office to identify the suspects.

The four men were arraigned in Felony Court on a charge of conspiracy and violation of Section 382 of the Penal Code. Section 382, which made it a felony to bribe a participant in an amateur sport, was being given the equivalent of a test run. It had been passed into law following the Brooklyn College scandal, and it would be invoked again, dozens of times, within the next few years. The first indication of how the courts might treat such a crime came when bail was set at fifty thousand dollars, a figure that would have been considered high for a first offender in a case of armed robbery or felonious assault. The second indication came two months later, on March 10, when Judge Jonah J. Goldstein sentenced Aronowitz, Klein, and Levy to from fifteen months to two and a half years in jail and Rivlin to one year. Since all four had changed their pleas from not guilty to guilty on the day their trial opened, it can be assumed that the sentences would have been even harsher had the trial proceeded to a conviction. At the sentencing, Judge Goldstein noted that the four men were small-time gamblers and that the case certainly did not "represent a wholesale conspiracy." The firmness of the law, of course, would serve as a deterrent to others who might be similarly inclined.

Shapiro, quite properly, was loudly praised by both college officials and those charged with enforcing the law. Here are Hogan's words:

"The contamination of vultures such as these defendants can be effectively removed if other young men will follow the courageous course of David Shapiro. Under terrific tension over a period of months, he cooperated magnificently. He has rendered an outstanding service to sports and law enforcement."

Hogan's statement would probably not have been altered in the least had he known that within just five days prior to the arrests at least two games were fixed in Madison Square Garden. Before the year was over, Manhattan College would be fixing scores routinely, though not quite so regularly as other teams in the city.

But for the time, the slate, once again, was wiped clean. Shapiro had set the good example for college players everywhere. The "vultures" were sent off to jail as convicted felons. The sport was made safe again for clean-living American youth. The system works!

The law, of course, lives by its devotion to the idea of deterrence. It is a quite literal body, the law, and its machinery is tooled to operate only on the fuel of hard evidence. As a consequence, it is oblivious to the suggestions of nuance, to the soft shadings of truth that can sometimes be inferred by the very absence of evidence. The law has no ear for the unspoken dialogue. Therefore, the Shapiro case was marked closed with the sentencing of the defendants. That is the last stop on the line of legal procedure. The tracks run no farther.

But in the less formal court of the streets, the absence of evidence was building again. The age of the four convicts ranged from thirty-four to forty-three. It was not a case of some local kids acting on the impulse of a quick, easy score. Rivlin, in fact, had described himself to the police as a professional bookmaker. Three of the men, all but Levy, were residents of New York City. Yet, we were asked to believe, they found it necessary to travel two hundred and fifty miles to try to fix a game involving a team from Washington, D.C. And what a prospect they chose! They did not approach an eighteen-year-old kid from the ghetto who might be ready to gamble on the chance of a few quick bucks. They went to Washington to meet with a twenty-five-year-old war hero living on the GI Bill, a law student who might be expected to give serious thought before putting up his career as collateral for the sum of five hundred dollars. That was their selection. So if this was indeed not part of a wider conspiracy, we would have to believe either that Shapiro seemed the most corruptible of all local athletes to four seasoned gamblers, or that players on all the local teams had already snubbed similar offers and that not one of them, not a single one, thought to report it. Those were the alternatives, for here were the judge and Scotti of the Rackets Bureau agreeing that there was no evidence of wider scandal. The operative word was "evidence." To the law, evidence is the type of documentation that can be produced and accepted in a courtroom. But try telling that to the bookmaker at the Bickford's cafeteria in the West Bronx. Try telling him you like the underdog in that night's game with LIU at the Garden.

"So does LIU," he says.

"But where is your evidence?" you ask him.

His evidence? His evidence was that LIU had failed to cover the points three times in its last four games. That was the most tangible evidence he had to offer and therefore, in the logic of his world, the least trustworthy. For the rules of evidence of the streets operate in inverse ratio to those of the system. The prizes most cherished by the legal system—the signed document, sworn testimony, corroborative accounts—are scorned in the streets. They cannot be trusted: people lie, and it takes more than an oath to convert a liar to the truth. It is possible that no one is better tuned to the many colorations of truth and falsehood than a man who lives his life on the frayed edges of the law. Certainly there is no quicker nose for the first smell of scandal. It is fundamental to him, a matter of survival. He has no time to wait for evidence.

It is for that reason that such dialogue as takes place between the system and the streets is always conducted as an adversary proceeding, a process of dialectic which invariably leads each party to contrary conclusions. The system will recognize as true only that which can no longer be denied. In the streets, one learns to deal with muter tones. And so, legally at least, the latest scandal was laid to rest. There was no evidence of further conspiracy. It is the nature of law enforcement to be consoled by events that should alarm it, and to treat every suggestion of corruption as a further guarantee of innocence.

The men were reported, arrested, convicted. They went to jail.

The system works!

6

The next two years seemed to be a Golden Age of basketball in New York City, especially to a teen-ager who might still hope to grow a few inches and who had something of an eye for the basket and a touch for the ball. The New York teams had never been better, and the formation of the National Basketball Association served to quicken interest in the college game. Each year the best of the graduating seniors would be skimmed from the campuses to play for professional franchises around the country, and there was room to wonder which of the college stars would be good enough to make it. Melchiorre, for example, was near to being an All-American at Bradley, but at five foot eight would he be big enough for the pros? Would Roman be fast enough? Was Layne a sufficiently good shooter? So each college player who came into the Garden was scrutinized twice. Every kid with seventy-five cents and a student G.O. card in his pocket had become, in effect, a professional assessor of basketball talent. The entire sport seemed to be approaching a new level of proficiency.

But then each era in sports is probably the Golden Age to those who lived it through their teens. Would you not listen again and again to the stories that grew up around the Original Celtics and the

St. John's Wonder Five? Eyewitnesses were always ready to inform you that no one who played the game now was the equal of Nat Holman or Joe Lapchick. The old Celts would have eaten the City College grand-slammers for breakfast, more than one witness would attest. For time is the ritual that gives sports its life. Each passing year is an ornament that embellishes the feats of an athlete, until the lines in the box scores blur into memory and the agate type of one generation becomes the mythology of the next.

It will be that way always, for it is during one's teens that the dream grows brightest. Every street in every city neighborhood seems a runway that leads directly to the big time. To the three-sewer stickball hitter, the tenement in deep left field bears resemblance to the battlements of Yankee Stadium, and which schoolyard hotshot does not see nets beneath the cordless rims and hear the faint muddled music of the Garden on days when the feel of the ball is right and the basket seems to greet each shot with a new embrace?

So the 1950–51 season could be looked to with relish by a high school senior who yet harbored a vision or two. The calculations were made mostly in the polished nights of revery. The grand-slam sophs would all be seniors by the time you entered City College. You were not nearly of that caliber, you knew, but your ambitions after all were modest. You were just hoping to make the freshman team next year, and then perhaps be lucky enough, or hot enough, to survive the last varsity cut as a sophomore. It was not impossible. A realistic appraisal at age sixteen dictated the wisdom of goals that were not extravagant. Even if you grew several inches in the next few years, you would still not approach six feet. You had good, but not spectacular, speed, your floor game was no better than average, and defense was an accommodation you made to the rules of the game. In just the same fashion that Ted Williams played the field in order to qualify for his time at bat, so you played defense for the chance to shoot the ball through the basket. It was not the poorest hope on which to pin one's chance of making the varsity. Each man played only briefly during tryouts, and a hot shooter would certainly catch the eye of the coach more quickly than the best defensive player or a wizard of a dribbler. Yes, the final bet of the day might well be placed on the point maker, and if you were certain of anything at all it was that on a good night you could shoot the lights out in any building with a basket.

In the meantime there remained a full season and a summer in which to hone one's skills. The season would be spent on a free-lance basis. The coaches in the city high schools were on strike, and there were no varsity, junior varsity, or intramural sports. But when it came to basketball, there were other, less formal institutions of learning. There was a night-center league in Creston Junior High School, in the West Bronx, and it was run by Dick Kor, who played backcourt for NYU in the late forties. Kor was a ruggedly built, hard-nosed playmaker who gave away nothing on defense, and so he possessed precisely those skills one was looking to acquire. He also was generous with his time and advice, and he could teach you a great deal about cutting off the driving lanes on defense so you would not always have to play step for step with a man who might be quicker than you were.

But a good deal of what was needed could be learned right in the schoolyard, not only by playing but by watching. Admission could have been charged for the Sunday-morning games at Creston. Dick Kor could be found there, and Ed Roman, and Jack Molinas from Columbia. There were players from other colleges in the metropolitan area, and they were complemented by the schoolyard regulars, unknown names who, for one reason or another, never went to college but who could have played for any team in the city. They were the twilight people of city basketball, legends in their home schoolyard, and with reputations that carried into other neighborhoods but that were destined to endure not long beyond their last good game played on a concrete surface. For they would leave behind no record of their accomplishments, and immortality in sports resides in the epitaphs written in the very small type. Their names would remain part of the schoolyard lore for a while after they left, but then the texture of the neighborhood would change, and the people who saw them play would follow the line of their lives elsewhere, to other neighborhoods and other cities, and new schoolyard heroes would perhaps emerge to carve their own initials in the soft clay of remembrance.

But still, death did not come so quickly. Years later, one might yet share a memory with a new acquaintance at a cocktail party or even with a cab driver in Cleveland who went broke trying to tour the country as a pool hustler. You might have seen one or the other before, on brief passing occasions, but twenty-five years made it too long to remember. There was some gray in the hair now, and a drink in hand, and the twists of recollection, the reaching back across the years for names no longer attached to faces, made you realize just how long ago sixteen really was. You had children that age now!

But common ground would yet be found. Legends are grease for the memory, and neither of you would soon forget Bernie Grant, or Joe Green, or Herb Slovik. Grant was conceivably the best three-man basketball player you had ever seen. He was not more than five foot eight, but the crowd would gather when he went one-on-one with Jack Molinas, who was almost a clear foot taller. Grant played the game with a coiled intensity that seemed always about to crack him open. He would drive on Molinas with full contortions of body and face, every muscle wound as tight as a clock's springs, ready to pop on signal, no grace to his moves, no ease of deception, just a sudden fevered rush of precision, as quick and as sure as the knifing slice of a laser beam. He would burst past Molinas for the basket, and then, his head bobbing, his eyes taking in the reaction of the onlookers, he bounded with short mincing rabbit steps back toward the midcourt line, his hands hungry for the feel of the ball.

On Sunday morning, the games would often go to full court, and there was always the chance, if the game got started soon enough, that you might find your way onto the court. You would arrive early and immediately begin to take stock of the talent in the room. If there were eight good players present and a three-man game was at its end, sides might be chosen and ten players were needed. So you moved tentatively onto the court, with perhaps half a dozen your own age, and you waited for the moment when Molinas or Roman might look in your direction and say, "I'll take him."

The pace of the game would be brutally swift and its mood was serious, and there were times when you felt as though you had wandered onto the court by chance. The game seemed to be going on all around you, the ball streaking past your head, you did not know where on the court you ought to be, when to move or when to hold your position. You would cut for the basket, and finding the traffic heavy, pull up and a pass fired in your direction would whistle by and go out of bounds.

"When you start for the basket keep on going," Kor instructs.

"I didn't think you could get the ball through," you tell him.

"I can get it through," he says with a glance.

And then you try the same maneuver and this time you keep going, and somehow the ball is there, right past your ribs and into your hands and you lay it in the basket. On the way back down the court Kor smiles his approval, and you understand the truth of the old schoolyard injunction, "When you play with shit, you look like shit." You have to get in over your head.

So the year would be spent that way; each afternoon and every weekend, twice a week in the night center; thirty, maybe forty hours a week of basketball, always hoping to get chosen into one of the big games. You could learn what you needed to know that way, the simple moves, the rudiments that must be acquired but that can never be taught: when to break for the basket, when to set a pick, when to shoot and when to pass. The body learned those things gradually, it learned to react to silent, almost invisible cues, and you knew now that much of what was later called instinct was the product of one thousand hours of learned response.

But the longer one played and the more one learned, the sharper became the perception of limits. The radius of one's potential is widest in those areas that are left untried. Now you had played enough to know that you would never be able to funnel the ball through narrow channels the way Kor could, you would never be able to mount the fury of Bernie Grant's drives to the basket, no quantity of time spent on the court or at a blackboard would ever grant you the skills to put the latch on a truly first-rate player. It was not all learned response after all. The really good ones brought some of it with them. So it was still too early to lay the dream away, but it was not unwise to suspect that the dawn might come sooner than one had hoped. No, there was not the slightest chance that you would ever be a college star, but it was still possible that in two years you would be good enough to play for City College. You could still hope to earn a varsity letter, and be coached by Nat Holman, and—sweetest of all dreams now grown to adolescence—you might one day play a game of basketball in Madison Square Garden.

It was with just such a hope, not immodest but sufficiently ambitious, that one looked forward to the season of 1950–51. City College would be defending its twin titles. The sophomores were all juniors now, and you could not begin to estimate just how good the team might finally become. St. John's would certainly be as tough as it was the previous year, and LIU—with Sherman White, Adolph Bigos, and LeRoy Smith—might be better than either of them; might, in fact, be the best team in the nation. Then there was NYU, with the promise of strong sophomore talent, and Manhattan College, which would compensate for the loss of Hank Poppe and Jack Byrnes with the addition of a six-foot-eight center named Junius Kellogg.

The prospects, then, were bright indeed, and one cast an eye to the future with the wistful longing of a would-be lover awaiting his turn. There was no way to know then that the day was closing for all of us. The last season of its kind in Madison Square Garden, perhaps for a lifetime, began like most others on November 25, with City beating St. Francis and Seton Hall defeating Rhode Island.

City followed with a routine victory over Queens and an impressive two-point decision over a powerful team from Brigham Young. It appeared that momentum was carrying over from the previous season. Roman averaged twenty-three points and Warner twenty for the first three games, and Roth and Layne were playing well. The Beavers had won twelve straight games spanning the two seasons, and they were heavy favorites coming up to their game with Missouri. But they were beaten badly, by seventeen points. City managed to score only twelve baskets from the floor in sixty attempts—an incredibly low 20 percent—for a game total of thirty-seven points. Roman, Layne, and

Roth missed repeatedly. Warner was high with only eleven points. Roman, Roth, and Arnie Smith all fouled out. It was the team's worst showing in two years.

They bounced back against Washington State, but then lost to Oklahoma as they had a year earlier, almost to the day. Warner injured his knee and ankle against Oklahoma, and missed the Brooklyn game, but he wasn't needed. Roman scored thirty points, a new Garden record for a City player, in an easy 64–40 win. However, Warner might have made the difference in the three-point loss to Arizona that followed. He played only two minutes, resting his leg for St. John's, but it did not help much. He was still not at his most effective, and St. John's beat CCNY 47–44. It was not an upset. By all accounts, St. John's was the superior team that season. At the mid-January break for final exams, about halfway through the schedule, the Redmen had a record of eleven and two, their most recent victory being a nine-point decision over undefeated and number-one-ranked Bradley. City had won only six of its eleven games, and the team had not looked really good since its game with Brigham Young.

But even St. John's was not the best team in the city at that stage of the season. That distinction, without qualification, belonged to Long Island University. LIU's record stood at 12–0, and only three of its games had been close. The Blackbirds had beaten UCLA by nineteen points, South Carolina by twenty-six, and Duquesne by thirty-two. Sherman White was averaging well over twenty points a game, and his best nights seemed to come against the strongest teams. He had already put together games of thirty points against Western Kentucky, twenty-nine against Duquesne, twenty-six against UCLA, and twenty-four against both St. Louis and Bowling Green. White was very likely the best college basketball player in the country, certainly its leading scorer, and he was anything but a one-man team. Playing with him were LeRoy Smith, a speedy, quick-handed playmaker who could also get his twenty points in a game, and Adolph Bigos, a balding World War II veteran who rebounded with strength and consistency from his forward position. The other guard spot was filled by Hal Uplinger, and at center was a six-foot-eleven sophomore named Ray Felix, who later would play for the New York Knickerbockers.

LIU might have been the best team in the nation, but it was barred from the NCAA tournament. The NCAA, the National Collegiate Athletic Association, closed its doors to LIU because of its questionable policies of recruiting and subsidizing athletes. It violated what the NCAA modestly called its Chastity Code. For that reason, too, LIU did not appear on the schedules of most of the other local colleges. It was, in a sense, a renegade team, an outcast even in the netherworld of gamblers and bookmakers, for all through the season there was virtually no action to be had on LIU games.

The rumors were everywhere that fall and early winter. One did not have to be a bettor to hear them. Other teams were suspect, they were maligned in whispers, but it was simply taken as fact that LIU was shaving points. These were not the usual rumors. One grows accustomed to cries of "fix" from smart-money bettors who have tapped out on the favorite. But now it was the bookmakers who were putting the finger on LIU, and there is no more reliable source in the world of sports. To a bookmaker, a fixed game is a greased chute to oblivion. He would sooner place his stake against a loaded pair of dice. For professional bookmakers are not gamblers; they are businessmen. They operate, in the best tradition of the entrepreneur, on the principle of selling their services for a sum slightly higher than cost.

The point spread is set at a level calculated to make both sides equally attractive. Then each bettor is required to put up eleven dollars for every ten dollars he hopes to win. The extra dollar is the bookie's vigorish, his margin of profit, the equivalent of a salesman's commission. In order to assure the profit, he must come very close to distributing the action equally, so that a like amount of money is bet on each team. In that way, he receives eleven dollars on every losing bet and pays out only ten on each bet won. The difference is his; he lives by the vigorish. The system, however, is not without its risks. When more money is wagered on one team than on the other, the point spread must be adjusted to compensate. If a six-point favorite, for example, is being bet heavily, the spread might rise to seven or eight in order to make the underdog more attractive. But when big money begins coming in on the underdog, a bookmaker might be given to panic. He will try to "lay off" some of the money, to transfer some of those bets to other bookmakers, but if the action everywhere is on the underdog there will be no one to take it. Nor will adjustments in the point spread prove effective. Too sharp a drop will only stimulate further action in the same direction. It would be the equivalent of the impulse to sell when the bottom seems ready to drop out of the stock market. And if the favorite is going to lose the game outright, there is nothing that can be done to right things. It will be a bear market, and the bookmaker will be obliged to take his loss. So the bookmaker, as devout a capitalist as the head of an oil cartel, is ever alert to the first suggestion of a fix. And if the evidence is substantial, he exercises his capitalist's prerogative; he pulls the game; he takes no bets at all.

This is what had been happening all season with games in which LIU was a participant. LIU had been consistently under the points early in the season, and large sums of money were coming in on the underdog from as far away as California. The evidence, though circumstantial, was compelling. LIU was winning big in the games in which it was favored by narrow margins. But its one- and two-point victories seemed to come always in games that it was expected to win handily. The implication was clear. Since it was next to impossible to shave points and still win a game in which the spread was small, LIU set no restraints and won by as much as it could. But when the points ran as high as seven or eight, it might not be too difficult to win the game and still stay under the spread. It might have been coincidence, but the pattern was unmistakable.

So the foul air of scandal hung like menace over the first months of the 1950–51 season. It was spoken of openly in the corners and crevices of the New York streets, but it was treated as a private matter among more official sources, the tasty little tidbit of inside gossip that is acknowledged only with a wink.

The first thin splinter of the story was pushed into the open on

January 10 by Stan Isaacs, a sports writer for the now-defunct New York *Daily Compass*. Bookmakers, Isaacs wrote, have been shutting off bets whenever a "certain local team" was playing. He did not name the team and he did not name the contact man, but he gave reason to believe that his knowledge was intimate. He said the contact man was a former player, "one of the biggest names in collegiate basketball a few years ago." There had always been doubt about the games in which he himself had played, Isaacs wrote, because of his hot and cold performances.

And conceivably the name of Jackie Goldsmith, formerly of LIU, occurred to more than one reader whose memory reached back to the mid-forties.

The column was not of the sort to delight a coach. Coaches, after all, are a part of the structure; they have a basic trust in the hard coin of evidence. And so exactly one week later, on January 17, Isaacs reported that the coach of that "certain team" (presumably Clair Bee) had shown him the column and advised that he shouldn't be writing "stuff like that," that it was not good for the game.

"Unless someone starts writing 'stuff like that,' " Isaacs retorted, "something's going to break that won't be the least bit good for the game."

"When something happens," the coach said, "then talk to me."

By the time the story appeared, something had already happened.

What happened was that five men, including two former Manhattan College players, were arrested early that morning, on January 17, for trying to fix the score of the Manhattan–De Paul game in the Garden. The two players—Hank Poppe and Jack Byrnes—were the stars and high scorers of the previous season. The other three were professional gamblers. Their arrests followed the attempt to bribe Junius Kellogg to fix the previous night's game with De Paul. Kellogg reported the offer immediately and cooperated with the police in helping to trap the suspects. To first appearances, it seemed a repeat of the Shapiro incident two years earlier. But Poppe, who was the contact man, made what the police termed a "complete confession." The confession included the information that he and Byrnes had dumped three games the previous season. They also had accepted money to try to exceed the point spread in two other games. And there was something else that Poppe said. It was uttered as part of a lament, but it carried with it the worst of portents for the coming months. "Why did they have to catch us," he said, "when so many other guys are doing it? This has been going on for years."

So it was breaking now. There was every reason to believe that this was just the first crack in the pipes. Now it would start oozing to the surface, seeping through the drains and conduits like the backed-up waters of a cesspool. It would take a while, of course, but who could guess just how deep it ran, how much Poppe knew, and how much of it he would reveal? He already had confessed. He faced a felony conviction. It was part of the machinery of the courts that information could be traded for time. Poppe had cause to tell everything he knew. ". . . so many other guys are doing it," he had said. "This has been going on for years."

The initial confession covered five games played during the 1949–50 season. On December 3, 1949, Manhattan was a four-point favorite over Siena, but lost the game 48–33. On December 29, they lost to Santa Clara 73–64 after entering the game a two-point favorite. Manhattan was a seven-point underdog to Bradley on January 12, 1950, but succeeded in losing the game by twenty-two points. Then there were two games later in the season in which Poppe and Byrnes were able to help Manhattan exceed the spread as favorites against St. Francis and NYU. Byrnes and Poppe were paid one thousand dollars apiece for each of the five games.

The three men accused of bribing them were: Irving Schwartz-berg, thirty-six years old, of Elmhurst, Long Island; his brother Benjamin, a year younger, of Brooklyn; and Cornelius Kelleher, also thirty-five, of the Bronx. They were not small fry. The Schwartzberg brothers, at least, had solid credentials. Benjamin had been arrested eleven times, with six convictions, since 1932, when he was sent to the House of Refuge as a juvenile delinquent. In 1935 he had been sentenced to two and a half to five years in Sing Sing on a burglary charge. Four convictions for bookmaking followed—two in 1943, one a year later, and another in 1948—for which he was successively fined the sums of twenty-five, fifty, one hundred, and one hundred and fifty dollars. He also was wanted for questioning by the Forgery Squad. His brother showed a record, beginning in 1930, of fourteen arrests with eight convictions, mostly for bookmaking, but he also had served a prison term on a felony charge. Both brothers were remanded to jail. Poppe, Byrnes, and Kelleher, who was said to be the original contact man, posted bond and were released.

Kelleher had approached Poppe and Byrnes before the fall season of 1949 and guaranteed each of them forty dollars a week, as a retainer, if they agreed to control the scores of games. They both accepted, getting the retainer plus one-thousand-dollar cash bonuses for each game successfully fixed. It can be said in behalf of Kelleher and the Schwartzberg brothers that they dealt with the players fairly. They were paid their money regularly, promptly, and in the agreed-upon amounts. This would not always be the case in dealings between gamblers and players. Byrnes and Poppe, in their turn, always came through as expected, whether shaving the points or trying to exceed them. They were exceptionally gifted players, possibly the best ever to play for Manhattan.

Byrnes, a six-foot-four forward, could shoot with either hand and was an agile rebounder. He was a graduate of Xavier High School and he came to Manhattan with All-America promise. But his career was without luck. Twice he broke his leg, missing substantial portions of each season. Still, he was able to close his varsity career with a total of 893 points, third best in the school's history. At the end of his senior year, in June 1950, Byrnes was three credits shy of graduation, but he elected not to return. He wanted to play professional basketball. He was drafted by the Knickerbockers, but was cut before the season began and was playing in the Eastern League at the time of his arrest.

Poppe was a muscular six-foot-two guard who served three years with the Marines in the South Pacific before being graduated from Seton Hall Prep. He scored more than one thousand points at Manhattan, second only to Bob Kelly, and was graduated in 1950 with a degree in physical education. He played for a while in the Eastern League but was released early in November. He had signed up with the New York City Fire Department and was waiting to be called when he was arrested.

Both players were married. When their college careers ended, they found themselves cut off from earnings on which they had learned to depend. Poppe, after being released by the Eastern League, was living on funds paid to him under the GI Bill. If he had made decent money shaving points as a player, he might do as well or better acting as contact man. It was the next logical step.

"Look," he said later, "I was married . . . my wife was pregnant . . . I just got tired of eating hamburgers and hot dogs."

So he renewed his acquaintance with Kelleher and the Schwartzberg brothers. The De Paul game was selected for an outright dump. De Paul was a solid ten-point favorite, but the gamblers would wager that they would cover the points. Junius Kellogg, the six-foot-eight sophomore center, the first black man ever to play for Manhattan, would have a bad night.

Poppe visited Kellogg in his dormitory room at 242nd Street and Spuyten Duyvil Parkway in the Bronx on January 11, five days before the game, and offered him one thousand dollars to guarantee the loss. Kellogg was surprised to see him.

"Poppe had never spoken to me before," Kellogg recalled years later. "I had scrimmaged against him for a whole year and he never even said 'Hi.' Now, after graduation, he comes to my room and says, 'I've got a proposition for you.' And then he spelled out what it entailed. I was shocked. I told him no, but he said I should think about it for a few days and he would call me Sunday. I was really pissed," Kellogg said. "I was rooting my heart out all last year and this son of a bitch was dumping."

The next day, Friday, Kellogg reported the incident to Coach Ken Norton, but he did not name Poppe.

"I just told him that one of his ex-ball players had offered me a bribe," Kellogg said. "According to the rules I was supposed to report it. So I told Kenny, and then I forgot about it."

Norton did not forget about it. He called a friend of his, Police Inspector Abraham Goldman, of Brooklyn, and Goldman advised him to notify Deputy Inspector Edward Byrnes, chief of detectives in the Bronx. So the wheels were set in motion.

Manhattan had a game that Saturday night against St. Joseph's in Philadelphia. The next day, on the way home, Norton asked Kellogg to meet him in his office. Waiting there were representatives from the district attorney's office and Bronx detectives. They asked Kellogg to explain exactly what had happened. This time he named Poppe, and he agreed to continue with negotiations.

Poppe called again that night. They arranged to meet at a parking lot near the college campus. Kellogg walked there and arrived at about nine o'clock. It was raining and he was jittery. He waited for about fifteen minutes, his collar turned up against the rain and the cold, and then Poppe drove into the lot. He parked the car, and they crossed the street to a bar at Broadway and 242nd Street. There, over drinks, Poppe went into some detail.

He told Kellogg that players on other teams, both in and outside of New York City, had been getting money to fix the scores of games. And he explained something of the fine art of dumping. You miss an occasional rebound, he said, you don't try too hard to block shots, you slow up on the outlet pass so the fast break loses some of its effect. "Above all," Poppe told him, "don't stink up the joint." It could not be made to appear too obvious. Kellogg agreed.

They met again the night of the game in the lobby of the Belvedere Hotel, on Forty-ninth Street, opposite Madison Square Garden, to arrange the details of the payoff. It would be made after the game in the men's room of Gilhuly's bar on Eighth Avenue. Kellogg, who was wired for his meetings with Poppe, passed the tapes on to the police.

Kellogg had a bad night against De Paul. He played for only a short time and scored four points. But his replacement, Charlie Jennerich, hit eight for eight from the floor, added a foul shot for a total of seventeen points, and Manhattan upset De Paul 62–59. It would not be the last time that a substitute would come off the bench to turn a fix the other way. It was, to the gambler, an occupational hazard. Detectives followed Kellogg to Gilhuly's bar after the game, but Poppe did not show up. He was arrested early the next morning at his home in Flushing. Byrnes, who was not involved in the attempt to bribe Kellogg, was picked up two hours later at his Jackson Heights residence.

The two former players and the three gamblers were booked on charges of "conspiring to commit a crime of bribery in violation of

Section 382 of the Penal Law." More than a year later, on pleas of guilty, Kelleher and the Schwartzberg brothers were each sentenced to a year in jail. Sentenced with them, to a ten-month term, was Soll Leon Rappaport, an associate of theirs, who had managed to elude the police for almost two months. Byrnes and Poppe were given suspended sentences and were released on probation.

Kellogg, of course, emerged a national hero. He received a roaring tribute in a rally at the Manhattan College Quadrangle. New York City Police Commissioner Thomas F. Murphy awarded him a scroll of honor. He was commended by the City Council of his native city of Portsmouth, Virginia. The Chicago CYO Club of Champions presented him with its medal for "outstanding effort in the cause of youth" at the annual dinner of the Midwestern Sports Writers and Sports Broadcasters. Previous recipients included Babe Ruth, Jackie Robinson, and General Dwight D. Eisenhower.

The tributes were not undeserved. Kellogg had, in truth, committed an act of some consequence. David Shapiro, too, had reported a bribe attempt, but it was an isolated incident that involved no other players. Kellogg was blowing the whistle on a former classmate, and he had to suspect that it might be just the beginning. Poppe had indicated that the fixing of games was widespread. He told Kellogg that he and other players had been dumping games the previous season. The investigation was certain to proceed further. He could not at the time begin to guess its limits. And so he was prying open the lid on a package whose contents were entirely unknown.

"I didn't know it would become a national scandal," Kellogg now says. "At the time I didn't even know that Byrnes was involved. Poppe told me there were other teams in on it, but he didn't name names. But I still had second thoughts about it. In the ghetto, you know, they had this thing about talking, about turning people in. And I thought about Poppe too. He was married, and I knew what this would do to him. But I thought about my scholarship too. I weighed the whole thing. The rule was I would lose my scholarship if I didn't report it."

The scholarship, the chance to go to college, meant a great deal to Kellogg. He was one of eleven children, and he grew up in very modest circumstances in the small town of Portsmouth, Virginia. He attended I. C. Norcom High School, where he played football and ran track, but where basketball was a virtually unknown sport. The high school did not even have a gym, but an outdoor basket was erected during Kellogg's sophomore year, in 1941.

"I had never even seen a game of basketball played before," Kellogg recalls. "But I was already six foot four as a sophomore, and I spent a lot of hours at that outdoor basket. In two years I picked up enough to get a basketball scholarship to West Virginia State."

After a year at West Virginia State, Kellogg was drafted into the Army, and it was in the service that he really learned to play basketball.

"I met some pretty good players there," Kellogg says, "both at Camp Lee, Virginia, and then at Fort Dix, in New Jersey. There were a lot of college players in the Army then, and I learned a lot from them and spent all of my spare time working out in the gym."

While at Fort Dix, Kellogg also was able to play for the Trenton Tigers in the Industrial League. The games were scouted, and by the time Kellogg was discharged from the Army, in 1949, he had received scholarship offers from no fewer than ninety colleges around the country. He chose Manhattan because he wanted to play in New York, on a team that played its games in Madison Square Garden.

Throughout his freshman year at Manhattan, when he could do nothing more than scrimmage because he already had played a year at West Virginia State, Kellogg heard not the faintest murmur of dumping.

"As far as I knew," he says, "everyone was giving everything. I never even heard it discussed. The summer before I played ball in the Catskills with Ed Warner, and Eddie Miller of Syracuse, and Ed Younger, who was a pro, and I never heard anything mentioned, not until Poppe came to my room that night."

So the biggest betting scandal in New York City's history was broken open by a big black man from the South who possessed a respect for the rules found most readily, perhaps, in those who are granted opportunities they do not necessarily expect. In the South, it must be assumed, the rungs that might lead a black man out of poverty were invisible in the early forties. The ghettos of the big cities offered, at least, examples that might be followed. Each neighborhood—whether in the poverty-ridden streets of Harlem or the lower-middle-class blocks of the Bronx and Brooklyn—had a subculture of its own, through which one could salvage some remnants of his own identity. There was no one more important in the big-city ghetto than the schoolyard slick or the accomplished pool shooter, and no one more respected than one who had made it big. If you came from New York, you would always have a local claim on some national hero. There would be someone from your neighborhood who had made it to the big leagues or was a football or basketball star in college. And always there was the swarming subterranean culture that resided beneath the subculture. There were the bookmakers and gamblers, the poolroom hustlers and the guys who banked them. There were men who wore bright clothes and drove big cars and who seemed to have a road map for every sharp turn and narrow angle that showed the way out. They knew the shortcuts, and you would learn them too. Survival depended upon it.

You learned about hustling all at once in Nat's pool hall when you played and beat a stranger for time—the rental price of the table—and then, just to keep things interesting, played for a buck a game. You held your own until the stranger looked at his watch, said he had time for just one more game and why not play it for a big pot? Why not? The table was paid for and you were a buck ahead. So you held his buck and anted up the five you had in your pocket, and the first time you missed, your money was gone. The stranger had somehow found a finer edge to his game. He ran fifty straight balls, quickly and without hesitation, saying nothing except, on occasion, "bank the nine," or "far corner," and then "rack 'em." The game took no more than ten minutes, and then, without a word, he stuffed the five bucks (a week's wages for a delivery boy) in his pocket and walked through the door. He was a small-time hustler and you were his willing student. You learned quickly; it was cheaper that way. And would there not be occasions when you gave lessons of your own, though with a basketball rather than a cue stick?

There was, then, no shortage of models to choose from. By the time you were sixteen you would have a feel for the markings on every exit that led the way out. You knew about hustling and shaving and smart-money betting, about marked cards and guys with quick hands and shooting dice on padded surfaces. What you had not seen you had heard about. It was part of the lore of the streets. There was still room for disillusion, but there would not be many surprises. The city streets offered a full education, right up through graduate school, and you could stay for as long as you chose. It was not corruption that set the city apart from the small town, it was variety; corruption was only a part of it.

It was not likely that Junius Kellogg received quite such extensive schooling, not in Portsmouth, Virginia. One is ready to believe him without reservation when he says he was "shocked" by Poppe's offer.

"You had no suspicions at all?" you ask him.

"Ab-so-lutely none," he says.

Kellogg, who bears more than a passing resemblance to Bill Russell, the former basketball player and now an NBA coach, recounts his story from a wheelchair in his office in lower Manhattan, where he serves as Deputy Commissioner in New York City's Community Development Agency. He has been paralyzed from the waist down since 1954, when he was injured in an auto accident near Pine Bluff, Arkansas. He was one year out of college then and barnstorming through the South and Southwest with some of the Harlem Globetrotters.

"We were on a two-week break when it happened," Kellogg says. The fingertips of each hand press lightly against one another as he relates the story. "We were preparing to leave on a tour of South America. Some of us decided to pick up some extra money by playing some games in cities that hadn't been on the Trotters' regular schedule. We were driving through Arkansas, right outside of Pine Bluff. Boyd Buie, the one-armed player, was driving and I was asleep in the front seat. The roads were bad, small and winding, and we had a right-wheel blowout. Boyd wasn't able to keep control of the car, and we turned over eight or ten times. I was the only one who was seriously injured."

Kellogg was completely paralyzed. The prognosis at the Veterans Administration Hospital in Little Rock was that he would remain that way. But after a year he was transferred to the Bronx VA Hospital on Kingsbridge Road, and he was placed on a four-year rehabilitation program. Kellogg worked hard eight hours a day for every day of the four years. Gradually, feelings and movement returned to the upper part of his body.

"I accepted the rigors of the therapy program the same as I had any athletic training schedule. I just did what I had to do, and I guess you could say I got the maximum that I could under the conditions."

Kellogg began coaching wheelchair basketball while he was a patient and continued after he was released in 1959. During the course of the years he has piloted the Bronx team to five world championships. He also has maintained contact with many of the players who were caught in the net of the scandal. He says there are no hard feelings.

"I'm still friends with a lot of those guys," he says. "They've paid their dues many times over. It should have been over and done with a long time ago. It's twenty-five years now. But I guess it never will be. People just don't forget that kind of thing."

No, it would not be forgotten; not in twenty-five years, not in fifty. Such events can be digested, they can be reconciled, but they are never forgotten. Six years after the players involved in the Brooklyn College scandal were expelled, none had applied for reinstatement, none had obtained a college degree. The Brooklyn coach, Tubby Raskin, said in 1951 that two of the players were doing fairly well but had found it very hard to get started. The other three had not begun to overcome the effects of the scandal. Yet that incident was small by comparison with what was to come. The Manhattan arrests were just the first tear in the fabric. It had not yet begun to unravel.

The district attorney's office was continuing with its investigation. Bronx DA George B. DeLuca said he was looking for the head of a national gambling ring. His assistant, Edward F. Breslin, said they were seeking a former college basketball star who had paid players to fix games during the 1949–50 season. The day after Byrnes and Poppe were arrested, two unidentified men were questioned for six hours at Bronx headquarters before being released. DeLuca reported that his staff had picked up rumors of an attempt to fix the Manhattan–San Francisco game during the 1949 NIT. The deal was to have netted some player fifteen hundred dollars, but it never was made, and San Francisco beat Manhattan 68–43 and went on to win the tournament. So it was under just such a veil of apprehension that the season continued.

LIU was still undefeated, and Sherman White already had set a metropolitan career scoring record when the team left on a western road trip near the end of January. Then, after a narrow win over San Francisco to make it sixteen straight, LIU lost four consecutive games in the space of a week. St. John's was in the middle of a twelve-game winning streak. It had a record of seventeen and two when its streak was snapped in overtime against Niagara on February 15. That same night, City, the season's big disappointment, was beaten by Canisius for its seventh loss against only ten victories. But if City had disappointed, another New York team had climbed, almost unnoticed, to national prominence. Columbia University, which did not play in Madison Square Garden, was undefeated in seventeen games and had won twenty-six in a row over the past two seasons. The difference in the team was a sophomore forward named Jack Molinas, who was leading the Ivy League in scoring.

Of course, the scandal was never far from the surface. Measures were being introduced at every level of government. The City Council set up a commission to decide whether city-financed colleges and secondary schools should be permitted to participate in games played off campus. Bills were introduced in both houses of the state legislature to double the penalty for bribing an athlete. Representative Louis B. Heller, a New York Democrat, asked Congress to set up a five-man committee to investigate the fixing of college basketball games to see if the gambling ring was nationwide.

The colleges too were at work. The president of LIU, Tristam Walker Metcalfe, invited the presidents of eight other metropolitan colleges to a meeting to discuss gambler corruption of college players. Only Brother Bonaventure Thomas of Manhattan appeared, and the two talked for about an hour. Ignoring the invitation were the presidents of Columbia, Fordham, NYU, St. John's, Brooklyn, City, and St. Francis. It did not matter. It was already too late.

On Saturday night, February 17, District Attorney Frank S. Hogan reported that a number of players were being questioned in a new game-fixing scandal. A spokesman for the DA's office said the case was just breaking. It involved two local colleges. The questioning continued all through the night. The announcement came shortly after dawn on Sunday. Six men had been arrested on charges of bribery. Three had conspired to pay the bribes, and three had accepted them. The three who took the money to fix the games were Ed Roman, Al Roth, and Ed Warner.

PART
THREE

There are events that are the rightful property of an entire nation. They become part of its collective consciousness and can be used as a common measure of the horrors and blessings of that small part of life which is not one's own. They are the events that create a transient unity among strangers because their effects are shared, suddenly and arbitrarily, in much the same fashion that passengers trapped in a subway car begin to intuit the common ground of their existence.

Probably, there is no one in the country beyond the age of forty-five who does not recall where he was and what he was doing when he heard that Pearl Harbor was bombed or that World War II had ended, and few in their twenties do not remember with some care and detail how they learned that John F. Kennedy had been assassinated. Such events reside, always, more in the future than in the past, for they open a door upon new possibilities. And they become personalized for the very reason that they belong specifically to no one.

In like manner, there are other events that belong only to a neighborhood and a time. They are finally written as no more than footnotes to the history of a nation, but in the small concentric turns of time and place they have the power to shape and define, to transform the psychic life of those who experienced them at first hand. To later generations, the basketball scandals of the fifties would be no more than a part of the folklore of sports, as remote as the Black Sox scandal during the World Series of 1919. But if you were growing up in New York City then, with a basketball tucked under your arm, shucking your way through the schoolyard circuit, through the concrete Madison Square Gardens of the boroughs, you would not soon forget how you first heard that the City College team had been fixing basketball games.

Since the announcement came from the district attorney's office in the early hours of Sunday morning, no news of the arrests was carried in the Sunday papers. You knew that City had beaten Temple by twenty-four points the previous night in Philadelphia, that Roman had scored twenty-five points and Warner and Layne sixteen apiece, that Bill Mlkvy (the Owl without a vowel) was high with twenty-six, but that was all. But long before noon that Sunday, the word was being passed through the neighborhood. It came to you in Nat's poolroom, down beneath street level on Burnside Avenue, while you bent over the pocketless green of a billiard table trying to adapt the metaphors of straight pool to the more demanding nuances of three-cushion billiards.

"Did you hear about Roman?"

"Sure, he scored twenty-five."

"He was arrested for dumping. Roth and Warner too."

"For dumping what, the NIT or the NCAA?"

"Three games this season—Missouri, Arizona, and Boston."

The white ball with the dot nudged its third cushion and then started its cross-table journey in the direction of the red, the angle already off by a full ten degrees. It passed the red ball with much room to spare and came to rest in the far corner of the table.

"Who told you?" you ask.

"Who told me? It's all over the place."

"But who told you?"

"It was on the radio this morning."

"Did you hear it on the radio?"

"No."

Then it was not necessarily true. Many years later you would stand at a bedside watching the electronic screen that measured the life still left in a faintly beating heart, the jagged lines flattening themselves out until there was nothing to be seen but the thin horizontal line with its little dot zipping from left to right, flat and lifeless as death, and in some blank space of your perception you would see the line flutter again, it would seem to move even as you knew that it was as silent and still as the heart itself.

There is some final gap in each of us that separates knowing from belief, and it cannot be bridged too quickly, for it is a space that does not exist in our faculties but in the more difficult dimension of time. Months, perhaps years, are required before one understands with certainty that death is final. Time must be paid for verification. And just so, with events more public and not quite so traumatic, first-source corroboration is needed. One must hear it from a voice on the radio, see it and feel it in the smudged ink on newsprint. Knowing it was not enough, you could not truly believe it until you could fathom its effects. So you would wait in the corner candy store that night until the morning papers came up, first the *News* and the *Mirror* with their big box type, and then the *Times* in more subtle shades, and there were the halftone photos, and you could recognize Roman immediately, towering above the others in his long, loose-fitting overcoat, his face full, his gaze as blank and as flat as sheared slate.

So now the details were there for all to see. A total of six men had been arrested and charged. In addition to Roman, Roth, and Warner, there were Salvatore Tarto Sollazzo, a forty-five-year-old jewelry manufacturer and ex-convict, who was described as a sure-thing gambler; Eddie Gard, a senior at LIU and a former basketball star whose eligibility had run out, who was Sollazzo's contact man; and Harvey "Connie" Schaff, a player from NYU, who was charged with offering a bribe to a teammate, Jim Brasco, to fix the NYU–St. Francis game on January 30. Brasco had declined the offer. Picked up later and held as a material witness was sixty-year-old Robert Sabatini, who was another of Sollazzo's contacts. Roman, Roth, and Warner admitted accepting sums of up to fifteen hundred dollars to fix the scores of three Madison Square Garden games during the 1950–51 season. City was favored in each of the games and lost them all.

The three players were arrested as they disembarked from the train on the return trip from Philadelphia after the game with Temple. Detectives Abraham Belsky and George Jaeger attended the Temple game under cover and returned on the same train with the team. As the train pulled into the station, Belsky, who was in fact the uncle of David Shapiro, and Jaeger made themselves known to Nat Holman. They told Holman they wanted to question some of his players at the station house. The players were booked at the Elizabeth Street Station in downtown Manhattan after hours of questioning. They were mugged at police headquarters and then taken to the Criminal Courts Building on Centre Street. The rounds from building to building were made on foot through the eerie first light of the late-winter dawn. Bail was set at fifteen thousand dollars each for the City players and ten thousand dollars for Schaff. All posted bonds and were released. Sollazzo was held without bail, and Gard, on his consent, was remanded to custody. His custody might well have been described as "protective," for Gard was a veritable storehouse of information. While it would never be clear just how much he told, his revelations were doubtless considerable. He served only nine months in jail of a sentence that carried up to three years, and his early release was based on his cooperation with the district attorney's office.

All six were arraigned in Felony Court before Chief Justice John M. Murtagh, who noted that he himself was an alumnus of City College. In setting bail Murtagh said that Sollazzo "appears to have corrupted these young men and brought disgrace on a great institution."

Sollazzo indeed had a record worthy of note, what police describe as a "long sheet." Beginning in 1931, he had been arrested on charges of grand larceny, armed robbery, and jewelry theft. He had been convicted twice and received sentences of seven and a half to fifteen years and one year and eight months to three years. He served five years in State Prison before being paroled. Conceivably his connections were highly placed. He lived at 115 Central Park West, the same building that was the home of Frank Costello, and the two were said to be not unacquainted. He also was reported to be on close terms with Frank Erickson, Lucky Luciano, Meyer Lansky, and the Moretti brothers, key figures in the mob of Joe Adonis.

Sollazzo had spent the summer of 1950 in the Catskill Mountain resorts of upstate New York. The Catskill hotels were a magnet for ball players, and other college students, during the forties and fifties. The hotels were scattered through small mountain communities like Monticello, South Fallsburgh, and Ellenville, about one hundred miles north of New York City, and most of them thrived for only ten weeks during the year, from the beginning of July through Labor Day. They varied in size and facilities. The big ones had private golf courses, and horses for riding, and boats for sailing and fishing. But most every hotel had its own swimming pool, tennis and basketball courts, game rooms for Ping-Pong and cards, and they all offered three meals a day, usually kosher, and big-name entertainment in the evening, all included in the standard weekly bill. It was known as the Borscht Circuit to entertainers, and more than a few of the best among them, Buddy Hackett for one, rode to prominence in the summer stock of the Catskills.

The clientele was drawn largely from the vast reservoir of the Jewish middle class in and around New York City. The suburbs had not really taken root yet. They were just beginning to grow in Westchester County and Long Island and northern New Jersey, and most of the middle class still resided in small but adequate apartments in the boroughs, principally in Brooklyn and the Bronx, in very specific neighborhoods that had names like Brownsville and Williamsburg and Claremont Park and Kingsbridge. A great many of them spent the summer, or some part of it, with their young teen-age children in the Catskills, or, as they often referred to it, in "the mountains." (Later generations might yet conjure visions of their grandparents living like adventurers for two weeks in the Himalayas or atop Everest. They were mountaineers, explorers! Most of them had, hadn't they, crossed an ocean to get here?) They would pack into their early model Chevys and Fords and make the two-and-a-half-hour journey along the winding strip of Route 17, years before the New York State Thruway or the Kwikway was blasted through rock to speed the trip. For two weeks in July or August they fled the sweltering heat of their concrete palace of a city and lived, it must have seemed to them, like foreign royalty. They roamed through open spaces and basked in the sun, they were fed well and abundantly, and in the evening, after they had dressed for dinner and had their hands stamped as proof of residency, they were treated to entertainment equal to the best night of the week on television.

They were the end of a generation, the very last of an era, with their Old World values and habits, their superstitions and folksy wisdom, utterly uninformed and yet profound. The medleys of Eastern Europe still blurred their speech, but they were able to find their way through the labyrinth of the world's most complex city and, in the summer, they were able to find their way out.

It might have seemed an unlikely setting for the hatching of gambling schemes and the fixing of basketball games. What recommended it, simply, was that a great many college players spent the summer there. The hotel staffs were made up almost exclusively of college students on summer vacation. They worked as waiters or busboys or bellhops, being paid small stipends and counting heavily on gratuities to earn a week's wages. During the summer of 1950, it was estimated that some twenty thousand students were employed by resort hotels in the area. Those on the working staff were paid an average of forty dollars a month, and they could expect tips ranging from five hundred to one thousand dollars for the season.

Most of the larger hotels also had basketball teams, formed presumably from among the staff, and they played an average of two games a week against other hotels in an informal Borscht Circuit league as part of the entertainment offered the guests. There were some five hundred basketball players on the payrolls of about fifty hotels that summer. It was not coincidental that among them was some of the best college talent in the country. For example, Grossinger's, one of the largest hotels on the circuit, had on its staff Sherman White, LeRoy Smith, Dolph Bigos, and Eddie Gard of LIU, Connie Schaff and Jim Brasco from NYU, and Zeke Zawoluk from St. John's. It was a unit that probably could have beaten any college team in the country. It was an all-star team. The players did not all arrive at Grossinger's simply by chance. They were, in effect, recruited with the cooperation of the colleges' athletic departments. It was part of the fringe benefits offered to athletes. They were helped to obtain jobs for the summer.

The better players did not carry many trays or wash a great deal of dishes. They were paid to perform less arduous chores. They helped establish athletic programs, they offered instruction, their duties were loosely defined. If the truth could be told, they were paid to play basketball, but that would have made them professionals and would have cost them their college eligibility. So they drew their salaries, usually about three hundred dollars for the summer, for the performance of indistinct jobs, and there was money to be made on the side as well. If they were not privileged to receive tips as waiters and busboys did, the Borscht Circuit provided other means of payment. The betting on the inter-hotel games was often considerable, and it was not unusual for a big-stakes gambler to offer a percentage of his winnings to be distributed among the players for a peak performance. Gamblers also were drawn to the Catskills. They too liked fresh air and evening entertainment. And the rates could be especially reasonable. There were late-night card games in the game room, and now and then a craps felt might be placed over the Ping-Pong table, and before morning a man who got lucky with the dice or who knew how to handle a fistful of cards might find that his week's vacation had been paid for by one obliging guest or another. The next day he would check into a different hotel.

Small-time gamblers played their own version of the Borscht Circuit. They toured the small and medium-size hotels, sitting in on friendly games of gin rummy or poker, winning a few and losing a few until, toward the end of the week, they had some notion of where the money was and which guests might be prepared to meet the ante when the stakes grew. There is no successful gambler who does not have more than fair credentials as an amateur psychologist. He can tell within the space of an hour which of the players at the table have come to lose. He does not need to know why. He is not concerned with the thrusts of unconscious motivation. He is a psychologist who deals only in symptoms. He lives on the sound percentage of the quick diagnosis.

A card player who has done some winning during the course of the week is the professional gambler's most coveted prey, for he comes to the table with the feeling that he is playing with someone else's money and therefore can afford to lose and not get hurt. He also might be convinced, once his cushion is gone, that the percentages are now in his favor, his luck is due to turn, and there is no one at the table to tell him that the cards have no memory. By the time he has gone into the hole he will not be playing for money any longer. He will be looking to salvage his pride, and pride is precisely the luxury that no gambler can afford. A true gambler has devotion for only one commodity, and it is not pride; it is money. Everything else, drives that motivate people in other professions—pride, power, the recognition of intellect—have no place in the life of a gambler; they are matters of indifference. At the end of the night he counts up, and then he knows how smart he is.

Salvatore T. Sollazzo spent much of the summer of 1950 at Grossinger's, in the company of Eddie Gard. Gard would be entering his senior year at LIU, but his eligibility as a player had expired. He would therefore make an ideal contact man. He knew the players on LIU and the other metropolitan teams. He would have some idea of who the prime candidates might be. He would be able to approach them casually, to feel them out; it would not be the same as talking straight business with a professional gambler.

At the beginning of the school year, Sollazzo invited Gard to his West Side apartment and spelled out the details. Gard would line up the players needed to be certain that a team would stay under the point spread. Sollazzo would be able to bet the game heavily, with a reasonable assurance of winning. Gard would get a percentage of the take. The players would be given a flat rate for each fixed game.

On December 5, immediately after City defeated Brigham Young for its third straight win of the season, Gard brought some of the players to Sollazzo's apartment. He wanted the fix put in for City's next game, four days later, against Missouri. The players would each receive fifteen hundred dollars if City did not win the game by six points or more. The details were explained with some care. Sollazzo might not have known it then, but the players were not all in need of very explicit instructions. Some of them had been fixing games the previous year for a different group of gamblers.

City lost the game to Missouri by a score of 54–37. The team played ragged basketball in the first half. Their shooting was off, their passes were uncertain. Missouri led 12–11 after the first twelve minutes and then reeled off seventeen points while City failed to score. The score stood at 31–14 at halftime. City tried to close the gap in the second half, but could do no better than play Missouri evenly. Their rhythm was broken. It was never recovered. Roman shot three for seventeen from the floor for a game total of seven points. Roth was one for nine with three points. Warner, with eleven, was City's high scorer.

The other two fixed games followed a similar pattern, with City playing a poor first half, then rallying but coming up short. Against Arizona, on December 28, City fell behind 26–19 at the half, then came back to lead 33–31 with ten minutes to go, and finally lost 41–38, with Arizona freezing the ball for the last four minutes. Roman made three of twelve shots in the first half and four of eight in the second to lead the team with nineteen points. Roth again had only three, shooting one for six. Warner, who had an injured leg, played for only two minutes.

Again, against Boston College on January 11, City trailed 36–30 at the half, shooting only eleven for forty-one. They made the same number of field goals in only twenty-five attempts in the second half, and led at one point 58–54. But Roman fouled out midway through the half, and the team lost 63–59. Roman scored sixteen points, Roth had eleven, and Warner missed the game entirely.

The fluctuations in the point spreads also reflected a pattern. City dropped from twelve-and-a-half to six-point favorites against Missouri, from nine to six against Arizona, and from thirteen to seven against Boston. The drops were unusually sharp. One can assume that substantial sums were being bet on the underdogs. It is conceivable that one or another of the players might have wagered a portion of his own take. Indeed, it would be difficult to believe that they did not. They were each paid fifteen hundred dollars for the Missouri game and one thousand for Arizona. For the Boston game, Roth and Roman were to get one thousand each, while Warner, who did not play, was to be paid five hundred. But the reports were that the players were not paid in full for the Boston game and were still trying to collect at the time of their arrest.

Still, the money they were paid could have pyramided rapidly. Even if they bet only part of what they were paid on the next fixed game, their total assets would increase geometrically throughout the season if they continued to double their bets. And there was also side money to be picked up from time to time. The players were paid "good-will bonuses" of five hundred dollars to exceed the point spread against Washington State and two hundred and fifty dollars to beat the spread against St. John's. They succeeded each time. Hogan said at least one player had wagered everything he received for the Missouri game on City to beat Washington State.

Boston was the last of the fixed games. Roth and Roman were on a five-day vacation at a Catskill Mountain resort the following week when they learned that Byrnes and Poppe had been arrested. There may have been no necessary connection, but if an investigation were to ensue there was no way to know where the next leak might be sprung. Roth said later that they thought of turning themselves in then. They finally decided against it, but they did agree to sever relations with the gamblers. There would be no more fixes.

The connection, if any, between the Manhattan College scandal and those to follow was never clearly established. Even the relationships among players and between players and contact men would remain vague. The first indications were that Roth had acted as liaison between Gard and the other City players. It seemed not altogether unreasonable. They had known one another since high school when they played on the same Erasmus team. But Roth denied being the intermediary. He said he did not even know Gard was involved until after the Arizona game. Whatever thread of chronology could be established came largely from Assistant District Attorney Vincent A. G. O'Connor, who led the investigation and conducted the questioning. But he would not, of course, reveal which of the players was his best source of information.

The relationship that appeared to be clearest of all was the one between Gard and Connie Schaff. Gard and Schaff grew up together in the Williamsburg section of Brooklyn. Gard was two years older, a schoolyard player of considerable reputation, and if it can be said that he was Schaff's hero, it was equally true that Schaff was his protégé. Schaff was brought up on basketball. His two older brothers, Sid and Stanley, were two of the best schoolyard players in a neighborhood that produced more than its share of college stars. Connie was a natural shooter, and Gard made him his private pupil. He taught Schaff to make the most of his scoring ability, and while Gard was providing the oil that made the LIU machine run, Schaff was setting records at Seward Park High School, scoring as many as fifty points a game.

At NYU he performed erratically and was dubbed Crazy Shot Schaff. He was a starter as a sophomore but was only the fifth-highest scorer on the team. During his junior year, 1950–51, he was kept on the bench for the first five minutes of each game in order to steady him, and as the season progressed he developed into a leading scorer.

Gard introduced Schaff to Sollazzo early in the season. Sollazzo was not impressed. He said he did not think Schaff was good enough to deliver. He insisted that other players be brought into the deal. Schaff apparently chose first to approach Jim Brasco, with whom he had played the previous summer at Grossinger's. Brasco turned him down. Schaff was given occasional handouts of twenty or thirty dollars and free entertainment to try to set something up. He was not especially successful. The only game he was said to have succeeded in fixing was on New Year's Day 1951 against Cornell. NYU was favored by four points but lost 69–56. In that game, Schaff reportedly crossed the fixer. He was promised three thousand dollars to distribute among key players, but there were no other players involved. Schaff kept all of what he was given. What he was given was nineteen hundred dollars. The final edge always stayed with the house.

The day after the arrests, Schaff and the three City players were suspended from classes indefinitely. At City, three thousand students attended a rally in the Great Hall, urging support for the team in its remaining three games. Floyd Layne and Ronnie Nadell were named co-captains, replacing Roman and Warner. The loudest "Allagaroos" were reserved for Layne, the only starter from the grand-slam team who apparently had not been taking bribes. He was raised to the students' shoulders and carried about in celebration. The City administration announced that the team would be permitted to conclude its season at Madison Square Garden but suggested that the games might be returned to the gym the following year.

Reaction from other quarters was as swift and equally unsurprising. Congressman Heller asked for a nationwide investigation and a ban on off-campus games. In Albany, the Republican majority leaders of the legislature, Senator Arthur H. Wicks of Kingston and Assemblyman Lee B. Mailler of Cornwall, introduced bills that would double the penalty for bribing amateur athletes. The bills had the backing of Governor Thomas E. Dewey. The City Council pressed for immediate action on its resolution against off-campus games for city colleges and high schools.

The academic establishment was no less quick to respond. The New York City Board of Higher Education formed a three-man committee to study the problem. The Eastern Collegiate Athletic Conference was weighing the prohibition of summer-resort basketball for all players at the ECAC's ninety-one member schools. Dr. Harry Gideonse, president of Brooklyn College, said he was considering abandoning the Garden, even though Brooklyn played only one token game there each season, against City. Several big-time basketball colleges announced they would schedule no future games at the Garden.

The most righteous waves of rectitude, of course, swept east from the great plains of middle America. Phog Allen, the coach of the University of Kansas, was among the very first to make the fine regional distinction between solid midwestern values and the festering corruption of the East.

"Out here in the Midwest," he said, "this condition, of course, doesn't prevail. But in the East, the boys, particularly those who participate in the resort hotel leagues during the summer months, are thrown into an environment which cannot help but breed the evil which more and more is coming to light."

Thus spake Phog Allen.

Adolph Rupp, Kentucky's coach, was another not to be easily fooled.

"I wasn't surprised," Rupp said. "The newspapers there quote odds and play directly into the hands of the gamblers." Asked later about his own team, Rupp would reply: "They couldn't reach my boys with a ten-foot pole."

(A ten-foot pole, it would be discovered, was not at all necessary. Rupp's boys had been dumping games for years, including the opening game of the NIT in 1949, which cost Rupp his chance for a double championship.)

Bradley took the most dramatic action of all. The players voted unanimously to reject a bid to the NIT. They would not come East to play in the Garden again. The disease, after all, might prove infectious.

(There were other reasons, perhaps more persuasive, that might induce the Bradley players to snub the Garden. They might not have wished to enter the jurisdiction of New York. For they had been fixing games for several seasons, both in the Garden and in their own Peoria field house.)

Even New York's sports writers did not always react charitably.

Milton Gross, who made at least part of his living picking games against the spread for the *New York Post,* asked that the players be "punished to the limit of the law." But even that would not be sufficient. Gross did not think they ought to be permitted to obtain a college degree even after they served their time. That opinion was expressed one week after the *Post* announced it would no longer publish the odds on the games. The spreads were not printed in boxed agate type as is the current fashion. They invariably formed the substance of the lead headline in the sports section, spread across the top of the back page. On January 5, 1950, for example, the headline read this way:

Books Make LIU 6-pt. Pick; NYU Rated 5 Over Temple

As subtle as that. And Gross was a premiere handicapper. At the beginning of 1950, he had beaten the spread twenty-two times in thirty-four attempts. A man could make a living with such a gift.

But now his voice too was added to the legions of those who craved retribution. The loudest cries, the most forceful recriminations came, always, from those who might have shared a token of responsibility. For their true yearning was not so much for justice, but for absolution. The players, the Garden, the sport itself might have been sullied, but the structure in which power resides would have to remain untainted. Therefore, it was necessary for those within the structure to believe that they could act from strength, that steps could be taken to guarantee that it would never happen again. For the nature of power is that it requires constant reassurance of its ability to control. And so its response was, in a way, inevitable. There must be new laws with stiffer penalties, punishment must be surer and harsher, the triumph of right must be absolute and total. The spread of Communism would be thwarted by the passage of the Smith Act and the Feinberg Law, its demise would be hastened by the confinement of Alger Hiss and the execution of the Rosenbergs. The structure knew how to deal with such a menace, it knew how to retain control. And if it could contain so pernicious and universal a threat as world Communism, certainly it would have little difficulty in dealing with a handful of college kids on the make for a fast buck.

So fingers were being pointed everywhere—at the Garden and the summer resorts and the evils that lurked always in the shadows of the schoolyards and the pool halls and the dark forlorn streets of the city. The feeling of shock and dismay rang like the bells of doom through the canyons of academe.

"I can't believe our boys could do such a thing," one school official commented.

"Why not?" asked a reporter. "You paid them for campus jobs they didn't work at; you gave them passing grades for classes they didn't attend. You bribed them to play for you; the gamblers bribed them not to play too well. What's the difference?"

The sense of shock was short-lived. It always is; it fades as swiftly as it comes. But those who live in anticipation are never spared. The real heartbreak was to be found out on the streets. There, among those who could not even express surprise, the news came with the suddenness of the fist of death. For death always falls hardest on those who have intimations of its coming. Their acquaintance is umbilical. It hovers at the edge of despair and resides finally in the depths of a bottomless dread.

And now the death watch had just begun. On Monday afternoon, three LIU players—White, Bigos, and Smith—were taken to the district attorney's office for questioning. The questioning continued throughout the night. Clair Bee, the LIU coach, stood vigil in his office.

"I had placed a lamp in the window of my office so that they could see it as they turned the corner when they came back," he recalled some time later. "But at six A.M. I went to the window and put out the light. They weren't coming back."

9

White, Bigos, and Smith did not return at all; not to LIU, not to big-time basketball. They were questioned through the night, for almost twelve hours, at the district attorney's office. When it was over, the three had admitted receiving $18,500 in bribes to control the points for four games during the 1950–51 season and for three games the previous season. By all accounts, the confession came principally from Bigos, which was no less than proper since he was the first to be drawn into the scheme. Bigos was twenty-five years old, a balding combat veteran of World War II who had earned five battle stars and a Bronze Star in the European Theater. He also was the captain of the team and a logical choice for Gard's first approach. He was not the scorer White was, nor did he possess the playmaking skills of Smith, but he was the team's leading rebounder and more, he was in a sense its leader and elder statesman. The games could no doubt have been fixed without Bigos's cooperation, but it is not likely it could have been done without his consent.

So Gard approached Bigos in January 1950 and introduced him to Sollazzo at a midtown hotel. They were each promised one thousand dollars to stay under nine points against North Carolina State on January 17. It was not easy. North Carolina State played poorly, and

LIU looked woeful, finally letting the game slip away, 55–52. White became suspicious. After the game he accused Gard and Bigos of lying down, of not feeding him the ball, and of playing in a "phony manner." Gard asked White to meet him in a candy store near the school. There, he told him that he and Bigos had been paid off and offered to cut White in. A few nights later, they met for dinner at Sollazzo's apartment. Sollazzo informed White that the games selected for fixing were the ones in which LIU was a big favorite, and all they had to do was to keep the points down. "It's not like you're throwing your college," Sollazzo told him. White was agreeable enough. The players received one thousand dollars each for the game with Cincinnati on February 2 and for the NIT opener against Syracuse. LIU was a strong favorite each time but lost both games by wide margins, 83–65 to Cincinnati and 80–52 to Syracuse. They had not yet perfected their art. The following season, they would do considerably better.

With Gard ineligible to play in 1950–51, White drew Smith, the new playmaker, into the deal, and they wasted no time in getting started. The fix was in for the first two games of the season. LIU, a seven-and-a-half-point favorite against Kansas State on December 2, won the game 60–59, and five days later, favored by only four over Denver, managed to win 58–56 in double overtime. On Christmas Day they delivered again, beating Idaho 59–57 after entering the game an eleven-point choice. The last rigged game of the season was against Bowling Green on January 4. LIU was an eight-point favorite, but Bowling Green played so badly that it was difficult to stay under the spread. LIU led by 37–33 at the half, which was fine, but Bowling Green could not make a shot after intermission, and the Blackbirds shot to a 51–40 lead after five minutes of the second half, and the margin grew to seventeen points with ten minutes left to play. The only way to get back under was to throw the ball away and relinquish control of the backboards. Bowling Green scored twelve straight points to pull within five, and LIU coasted to a six-point victory, 69–63, two points under the spot. The second half was played in so slovenly a fashion that the school administration received several letters complaining of the team's performance. (It would not be reckless to assume that the letter writers had wagered a few dollars on LIU.) The players of course understood that the Bowling Green game had been a fiasco. They decided that it was too risky to continue. They told Sollazzo that they wanted out.

Sollazzo asked them to reconsider. He wanted at least one more big payday. Estimates were that Sollazzo had been betting an average of thirty thousand dollars on each fixed game. At that rate he would have made three hundred thousand dollars on the seven LIU games and the three involving City. Now he was eyeing the LIU–Duquesne game. It was to be played on January 16 as part of a Garden doubleheader. The other game on the bill was Manhattan–De Paul. Sollazzo offered to up the ante, but still the players declined. Sollazzo was not convinced. He bet heavily, more heavily than usual, that LIU would not cover the points. LIU beat Duquesne 84–52. White, Smith, and Bigos scored sixty-four points among them. District Attorney Hogan said that Sollazzo took a "godawful licking" on the Duquesne game. It was not known how much he lost, but before the month was over it was clear that he was in financial trouble. He was, among other things, faced with eviction from his four-hundred-dollar-a-month apartment on Central Park West.

It is understandable that Sollazzo would go to some pains to retain the services of the LIU players. One could not want a better meal ticket. They had, given a season's experience, become masters of the craft of point shaving. Four times during 1950–51 they had accepted bribes to control the scores of games. Four times they had stayed under the spread and still won each of the games. It was an enviable record. That same season, City had lost every game it tried to manipulate. But then the two teams employed altogether different strategies. City, apparently less certain of its ability to control the rhythm of a game, seemed fearful of scoring too many points in the first half. They opened slowly, invariably trailed at the half, and then sought to close the margin with a flurry in the last ten minutes of the game. It was a strategy that never succeeded. Not once in two seasons, it would later be noted, was City able to win double—to win the game and still remain under the spread. LIU, by contrast, was working on a perfect season. It controlled the game on the most delicate balance of shooting and defense.

Against Kansas State, LIU, a seven-and-a-half-point favorite, led by five at the half, then surrendered the ball often enough to see the gap closed, but held on for a one-point victory. The Denver game was more difficult to manipulate. LIU was favored by only four points and trailed by seven at the half. It surged to a tie at the end of regulation time, played even in the first overtime period, and won by a basket, half the allotted margin, in the second. LIU was an eleven-point choice over Idaho, but it ran into a hot-shooting team. Scoring consistently from the outside, Idaho took an early lead and held it through most of the game. It did not appear to be the profit of largesse. LIU seemed unable to overtake Idaho until White scored from the pivot to tie the game with a minute and fifteen seconds remaining. Idaho then tried to hold the ball for a final shot but Smith stole it and drove the length of the court, scoring the deciding basket with forty seconds left in the game. White was held to seventeen points against Idaho, but he still was able to average almost twenty points a game for the four fixed contests.

Just hours after the arrest of White, Bigos, and Smith, LIU canceled the remaining four games on its schedule and announced an end to all intercollegiate athletics. The players, of course, were suspended immediately. Judge Murtagh set bail at fifteen thousand dollars each. White and Smith were released on bonds posted by professional bondsmen. The bail for Bigos was provided by his mother. Supreme Court Justice Samuel H. Hofstadter declined bail for Sollazzo, saying, "I can hardly see a more despicable crime—the corruption of youth at the very fountainhead."

The players involved were indeed at the "fountainhead." White unquestionably was the best college basketball player in the country. He already had been named Player of the Year by the *Sporting News* before the scandal broke. He was certain to be the regional draft choice of the Knickerbockers when the season ended. Months later, he termed his involvement in the scandal "the greatest mistake of my life." "I'd had so much," he said. "People liked me, they came to see me play and they enjoyed meeting me. My girl was proud of me and so was my family. I was doing what I liked best in the whole world and the chances were good I could have kept on doing it for years. I might have been able to make as much as one hundred thousand dollars playing pro ball and then I could have spent the rest of my life coaching kids, enjoying the work and doing some good. For the sake of a few thousand dollars and some smart talk, I pitched all that away."

Neither White nor Bigos appeared to be in urgent need of funds. White's family lived in Englewood, New Jersey, where his father worked as a refrigeration engineer. Bigos was receiving benefits under the GI Bill. His mother, a widow, owned a grocery store in Perth Amboy, New Jersey, and, according to his brother Ted, the family was "fairly well fixed." Smith, by contrast, was not so well fixed. He worked in a garage after school and on weekends in order to meet his expenses. It had never been easy for Smith.

"There was all that money," he said, describing the temptation, "more than I had ever seen before in one piece in my life. I guess it's too late to be sorry . . . and I don't blame anyone except myself."

The only other person he might have blamed was White, his closest friend and roommate. Smith had never met Sollazzo. He was not approached by Gard. He was invited into the arrangement by White, who no doubt believed he was doing his friend a favor. He also might have reasoned that the games would be easier to control with the help of the team's playmaker. Three players—the center, a forward, and a backcourt man—were an ideal combination for the fixing of a game. The gamblers knew that. They rarely considered a game to be secure with fewer than three players under contract. There were too many ways it could go wrong. One hot player—even a substitute—could put a game out of reach in a matter of minutes. It could never be certain, of course, but a gambler, like any good businessman, knew the virtue of reducing his margin of risk. He also knew that the right three players were quite ample to get the job done. Not every coach was as knowledgeable. Clair Bee, questioned about the possibility of game fixing early in the season, noted that he was quite sure that it could not be carried off by just a few players on a team, and certainly it could not escape the attention of the coach. In fact, he considered the very possibility of rigging a basketball game to be rather remote.

"I've got good boys on my team," he said, "and I can't imagine that any of them would as much as speak to any of the shady characters who roam around the West Side. . . . But if, in another era, I were coaching another team that was less ethical, and if one or more of these theoretical players were to have been fixed by gamblers, I think I would know it. I would see a man doing something I knew he never did, and I would make one of two conclusions: (a) I would think he was sick and off his game; (b) I would think that some mental handicap—and in wild theory, it could be interference by an outside person, say, a gambler—was accomplishing the same result.

"Whatever the cause, I would substitute for the boy, wrap him up, and sit him on the bench. I might put him in the game again, but, as sure as shootin', if I noticed any more departures from form, I would take him out and keep him out.

"In my opinion, no one player, or even two or three, can throw a basketball game. The coach, however, could do it. How? By keeping the best scorers on the bench. By making a series of wrong decisions on personnel. By giving his team the wrong defense. By failing to provide effective measures against the opponent's big scorer. In a dozen ways.

"We are lucky to have an honorable group of men in the basketball coaching field. So far, I have never had any doubts about any of them, and I am convinced that none of them ever has done anything except maneuver to win each game the best way he could."

There was no reason to doubt Bee's candor. Since his statement was made in an interview just a few months before the scandal broke, it is not likely he would have contended that only coaches could fix games had he known that his own teams had been fixing games for years. The case could sooner be made that the coach of a fixed team would be the last to give way to suspicion. For a coach is insulated from his players by the thin but impenetrable barrier that invariably separates authority from its subjects. It is a relationship fashioned along classical lines. Every coach is a sage and each of his players a disciple. Nat Holman, in fact, often addressed his players in the third person, referring to himself as the Master. "The Master was proud of you tonight, boys," he might say. "He couldn't have done better himself." Holman perhaps typified the relationship, but the variations were less than subtle. The sense of intimacy and respect that might link a player to his coach mix freely with the resentment that is produced by dependence. One is presented, for a time, with a surrogate father whose rules are as arbitrary and whose authority is as complete as the original. There are rewards and there are punishments. One is told when he can play and when he cannot, he is assigned certain responsibilities and is held accountable, he is fitted to a role and is expected to adhere to it without protest and without appeal. A college player might have fifty teachers in the course of four years, but he is likely to have only one coach, and there is no room for selection.

It is not irrelevant, then, that coaches invariably refer to their players as "my boys." "I've got good boys on my team," Clair Bee said, but when his frame of reference shifted from his LIU team to a "theoretical" team, he spoke of them as "players" or "men." Indeed, the relation between father and son is the archetype of that which joins coach and player, and if as a result the player is dependent, the coach is even more vulnerable, for he is open to betrayal. His success or failure depends entirely on the performance of "his boys," and so his stature tends to be reflective. Authority finally becomes dependent on its subjects.

The coach of a big-time basketball team could not, therefore, easily entertain the notion that his players were dumping. They might be having a bad night, for it was taken as certain that they were not the equal of their forebears. They might have failed to implement the strategies of the coach, for they could not be expected to quickly absorb the intricacies of his own mind. But they could not possibly be dumping, for if they were, they would not be selling out themselves, or their team, or their college so much as they would be betraying their coach, and that would be the spiritual equivalent of patricide. A coach could no sooner live with the suspicion that his players are in on a *fix* than the father of a junkie can acknowledge that his son is taking a *fix*.

(The fix is in, it takes! The line on the game is the mainline. One can adjust the outcome, he can shape reality. If things are not to his liking, he is not altogether powerless, he can do something about it. He can fix it!)

So if the sins of the father are visited upon the son, it can be inferred that the son is not entirely without recourse. He too might leave a small bequest.

Thus when it came to ferreting out corruption, the coach might not be the first to pick up the scent. Holman appeared to be somewhat less assured than Bee about the possibilities of deceit. "A coach," he said, "sometimes can detect strange things, but he cannot detect motive." Of course, Holman's observation was made after the fact, and if he was somewhat less shocked than Bee, he was certainly no less bitter. "I have no sympathy for them if they are guilty," he said of Roman, Roth, and Warner. And there is little indication that he offered them much during the next nine months.

The reaction on the campuses was a good deal more sympathetic. Rallies were held at City and LIU backing the players, and petitions were circulated asking that they not be expelled. City's Student Council executive committee passed a resolution that would have permitted the players to continue their studies until the litigation took its course. At LIU, students carried signs protesting the ban on intercollegiate sports. The City College Alumni Association retained Jacob Grumet, New York City Fire Commissioner and a member of the class of 1919, to represent the players. Grumet was a former judge of the Court of General Sessions, and he had been an assistant district attorney under both Hogan and Thomas E. Dewey. He advised the players to cooperate completely with the DA's office, and announced that they were willing to testify before the grand jury. Their only hope for leniency was to turn state's evidence.

Eddie Gard needed little encouragement. He had been questioned almost constantly, and shortly after he left the district attorney's office on February 26, another former LIU player, Natie Miller, was arrested for accepting fifteen hundred dollars to fix two Madison Square Garden games in 1948. Miller, who was married and a Purple Heart veteran of World War II, was studying for his master's degree at NYU at the time of his arrest. He was accused of receiving one thousand dollars to throw the December 4 game against Bowling Green and five hundred dollars for a game with Western Kentucky on December 30. LIU lost both games by respective margins of thirty-three and twenty-five points. Bowling Green set a Garden record by running up a total of ninety-seven points. Miller was released under bail of five thousand dollars, one third the amount set for the other six players, because Hogan said he was less apprehensive about Miller's showing up in court. He was the ninth player (including Gard and Schaff) arrested in the ten days since the scandal broke. It was spreading now, reaching even further back in time, and scattered reports of other fix attempts were drifting in from other parts of the country.

In New York, the investigation was proceeding rapidly. On the day Miller was arrested, the grand jury began taking testimony from city detectives and members of the district attorney's office. Sixty-eight detectives from various departments and commands were now assigned to the case on a full-time basis. Hogan noted that he expected it to spread much further. Miller, it developed, had not been paid by either Sollazzo or his agents. That meant, Hogan concluded, that another major fixer, probably a rival of Sollazzo's, might well be involved, along with an entirely new group of players.

10

The 1950–51 season was almost over now. It had begun with the brightest of hopes and the best of anticipation, and now it was being played out slowly, aimlessly, in the sullen ashes of its discontent. Invitations to the NIT were being circulated, but there were few left to care. A meager crowd of seven thousand turned out for the Garden doubleheader pairing St. John's with NYU and Manhattan with La Salle. A week later, there were even fewer in attendance for the traditional match-up between NYU and Notre Dame, the two teams that introduced big-time basketball to New York. The romance was over. The love affair between New York City and basketball had been tarnished by deception, and the city reacted with the indifferent hostility of a betrayed lover.

Such devotion as remained was turned from Madison Square Garden to Morningside Heights in upper Manhattan, where Columbia University was edging its way toward an undefeated season. Columbia was a small-time team by New York standards. It did not appear on the Garden schedule. Its home games were played in the university gym, which accommodated little more than twelve hundred spectators. But here was Columbia, undefeated in seventeen games—twenty-six over the past two seasons—ranked third in the nation, behind Kentucky and Oklahoma A&M, and just ahead of Kansas State and Bradley. Columbia was being led by Jack Molinas, a prolific sophomore who was leading the Ivy League in scoring. Molinas was a Bronx boy, a graduate of Stuyvesant High School and the Creston schoolyard, a street kid and a rugged schoolyard player with a wiry, tough six-foot-six frame, huge sure hands, and a splendid southpaw shooting touch. He had the talent and the scholastic standing to attend any school in the country. He chose Columbia. There, he would prepare for law school, become an All-American basketball player, and graduate to the NBA. His prospects, in both basketball and the law, appeared to be unlimited. He was a remarkably gifted athlete and possessed an intellect that was more than the measure of most. He also had a carefree, often zany nature, a taste for the bizarre, and a curious fascination for gambling and the uncharted world of white-collar crime. In the end, his achievements in both law and basketball would be rather modest. He would, instead, do long time in the penitentiary and meet his death finally, at the age of forty-three, with an assassin's bullet in the back of his head.

But that would be many years later. In 1951 his world was still cut to the precise dimensions of the basketball court. On February 22, Molinas scored eighteen points while Columbia continued undefeated in its eighteenth game, beating Army 61–47, before 4,850 spectators at West Point. That same night, City College resumed its own schedule against Lafayette.

It was an emotional night at the Garden. Only 7,493 paid their way in, but almost half of them were City students, the most ever to attend a Garden game. The student body rallied behind what was left of its team, and the "Allagaroos" were as loud and as ardent as they had been the year previous when a very different City team was playing for the NCAA championship. Who could say, in fact, that the stake was not higher now? Last year's team had competed only for a national championship. The team that took the floor now was playing for its self-respect, for the worth and honor of the students it represented. The principal hero, of course, was Floyd Layne, the only "straight" player left from the grand-slam team, the only one who had not succumbed. Layne, who played center on the revamped team, was greeted with swells of applause, and he responded as a hero should. He played the best game of his life. He scored fifteen points in the first half and finished with a career high of nineteen. City defeated Lafayette 67–48.

The locker room after the game was an odd mixture, both joyous and solemn. The victory over Lafayette brought with it a degree of redemption, but it was more symbolic than actual. Nothing had been changed really, none of it was undone. A makeshift team of substitutes had won a basketball game, but the specter of all that had occurred in the past week hung low and heavy, a deep dark shroud had enveloped the team and the sport, and redemption would not come quickly, nor would it be unattended by more than a taste of retribution. These kids, who now were heroes for a moment, knew that their brief careers would be played out in the shadows. They did not know how soon. They did not know that their season was, in fact, already over, that the traditional closing contests with Manhattan and NYU would not be played. For five days later, two days before the game with Manhattan, Floyd Layne was removed from the City campus by detectives from the district attorney's office. He, too, had been involved in fixing the games with Missouri, Arizona, and Boston College.

Layne appeared to be relieved as he was ushered from the campus. "Well, I was expecting it," he told the police. Layne quickly admitted receiving fifteen hundred dollars for the Missouri game, one thousand for Arizona, and bonuses of two hundred and fifty dollars for the games against Washington State and St. John's. He said he was promised fifteen hundred dollars for the Boston College game but never received the money. Layne took the detectives to his home on Prospect Avenue, in the Bronx, and led them to a flowerpot in the bedroom, where he dug out of the dirt $2,890 carefully rolled into a handkerchief. He had spent only one hundred and ten dollars of the three thousand he had been given. He was arraigned the following day, and the home of one of his relatives was used as security for the five-thousand-dollar bail.

In all, a total of $26,430 of bribe money was recovered. Roth had $5,060 in three envelopes locked in a safe-deposit box in a Brooklyn bank, taken out in the name of his mother. Others settled on less secure places of concealment. Bigos had $5,000 stashed in two sealed envelopes sewn into the lining of a sports coat that hung in the attic. White delivered $5,500 from an envelope taped to the back of a drawer in his room at the Carlton Avenue YMCA in Brooklyn. Smith dug out $1,030 from the toe of a shoe in the closet of his room at the Calvin Street YMCA in Newark, and an additional $900 was stored in a safe-deposit box in a Newark bank, in the name of his brother, Alfred Smith, Jr. Warner led detectives to $3,050 in tightly folded bills in a shoe box in the basement of his aunt's home, where he resided. Representatives for Roman brought $3,000 to the district attorney's office in two installments.

Hogan said the players would be permitted to retain the bribe money to pay for their legal expenses. He also said that no deal had been made to exchange information for clemency. That, of course, was only technically true. Clemency is very rarely promised; it is implied. And by now Hogan knew that there was still much work to be done. On the day Layne was arraigned, the term of the grand jury was extended for another month, and Hogan announced the imminent arrival from Florida of a second key fixer, a former LIU star who was involved in fixing games for a big gambler other than Sollazzo.

The arrest of Layne blew open the valves that until then had been locked and well tended. Now, the waves of scandal and corruption seemed to be coming from a source that had no bottom. So long as Layne had remained unsullied, there was something yet to hold on to. One could still cling, with however frail a grasp, to the illusion of incorruptibility. For ten brief days, Floyd Layne had been the symbol of the proudest street ethic of them all. He had stood his ground and kept his silence. For if he knew, or even suspected, that his teammates had been tampering with the points, he himself had resisted the temptation, turned his back on the easy money, and had not thought to turn in his teammates. If he had no suspicions, then he was something of a tragic hero, playing his heart out in losing causes while being duped by his teammates. Layne had become, without asking, the last custodian of a tattered vision. So when the news came of his implication, one felt twice betrayed, and there was small grace left for forgiveness.

Even twenty-five years later, many would recall the arrest of Layne with the bitterest taste of all.

"The thing I remember most vividly," said Marty Glickman, "was the shock of Floyd Layne being named captain and being carried on the shoulders of the students around City College, and then learning that he too had been dumping. That really shocked the shit out of me. Boy, that hurt. I had thought, here was one kid who stayed clean, who didn't get himself involved. And then to find out otherwise . . . It was sad, it really hurt."

Of course, there was little else Layne could have done. If he had been spared the initial blow and granted one last dance with the fading princess, he had in the end been forced to pay double. For he had been obliged to live for ten days in the worst sweat of apprehension. Every unknown visitor, every knock at the door must have stirred within him the cold broth of expectation. He would read in the paper one morning that White, Bigos, and Smith had been arrested. Six days later he would learn that Miller had been picked up, and he must have known, with all the certainty of dread, that his own turn would come. The grand jury had begun taking testimony. First it was the police who were called. The players would be summoned the following week, or perhaps the week after. What could they be expected to say when they were asked, as surely they would be, if anyone else was involved? Could they be expected to add perjury to charges of bribery and conspiracy? They had already agreed to cooperate fully. Layne could not have had a moment's peace those last days of February, and one would not envy his nights. He would know, for a time, what it was to live with the ghost of Banquo and the conscience of Raskolnikov.

Once Layne had decided not to turn himself in, to let the investigation run its course, he had drawn the net closed. The events that followed were inevitable. He would be named captain of the team, and he certainly could not decline the honor. If a campus rally were to be held, it was he who would be the focus of celebration, and he could not disclaim his being suited to the role without appearing to be the reluctant, the falsely modest hero. So he would be loudly and demonstratively hailed by his fellows, knowing all the while that he was not worthy of their acclaim and yet unable to demur without raising suspicions. Layne, then, was required to experience some of his very best moments while suffering inwardly in the clutch of his most private guilt. So if there was an element of deceit in the posture he assumed during those ten days, there was also a touch of heroism and more than a little pathos.

There also was some irony in Layne's being picked up after the others and being pressed into a masquerade. For he was the last and the most reluctant of the four City players to join the conspiracy. Layne had been approached by Warner and Gard in the fall of 1950, but it was not until December that he agreed to play his part. "You might as well get in on it," Warner is said to have told him. "Others will if you don't." It was, presumably, Warner's prompting that had coaxed Layne into the deal. Layne and Warner were long-time friends, and they exerted a good deal of influence on one another. They had played together at the Harlem Y and for a short time at Clinton. It was Layne who helped to persuade Warner to go to City. Warner was all-city at Clinton, and he had received scholarship offers from many colleges, including Fordham, St. John's, Scranton, Lincoln University, and LIU. He had chosen LIU and had begun freshman workouts when Layne spoke to him about switching to City. Layne had already made his decision. He would attend City if he was accepted. He told Warner that City had a fine basketball program and the prospects of an excellent team. Warner spoke next to Roman and finally to Bobby Sand, the assistant coach, who said that City would have a dream team and might even get to represent the United States in the 1952 Olympics. Warner finally agreed to join his friend and transferred from LIU to City. So while Layne, by first accounts, appeared to be the more resolute of the two, he was not, in the end, entirely immune to Warner's urgings.

Layne in fact was a curious mixture of moods. He seemed to be less certain of himself than he might have been, unconvinced even by his own accomplishments. He was a quality basketball player and an outstanding baseball prospect, but he was not sure he was good enough to play for Clinton. ("If you make the team at Clinton," he had said, "you're somebody.") He was a good, if not distinguished, student, and yet he considered himself lucky to be accepted by City. He said he wanted to work hard and earn good grades, and he attained close to a B average in his first two years. He was a sober student, with serious intent, and one of the best-liked players on the City team, lighthearted, easygoing, and quick to laugh. During the grand-slam season, he was the subject of a newspaper story that was titled "A Guy with a Grin."

Indeed, he was the most exuberant member of the team after it had annexed the twin titles. One remembers him grinning and almost giddy with joy, eager to share the credit with players and coaches, and almost everyone he had ever known.

"Hey, give that Bobby Sand a plug," he said when interviewed. "Hey, give Bill Spiegel a break. He's the coach at Franklin; taught me everything I know. Boy, what a coach! He's great. And that City! That's a great school; deserves anything it can get. Hey, give City a plug, too. Am I happy I went there!"

His big dark eyes were open wide and dancing with laughter. The contrast was thus all the sharper and more poignant that afternoon in late February when he was taken from the campus, a lonely model of deceit and betrayal. His eyes were blank then, and without focus, with the sad and wounded look of a fawn that had been stalked and cornered.

Just hours after Layne was taken into custody, City canceled the last two games on its schedule. Manhattan also ended its season prematurely. Only St. John's and NYU would play out the string. It was like staging an epilogue to a play that had lost its audience at the second intermission. The season was over and an era ended with it. The NCAA recommended that its members boycott Madison Square Garden. While the recommendation was not binding, the NCAA tournament would be played elsewhere in future years. What was left of the City College basketball team voted its preference to play the following season's games in its own gym, with a seating capacity of one thousand. Manhattan, NYU, and St. John's announced that they would continue to use the Garden, and the Garden management in turn took steps to attract a different clientele. Admission prices for students of competing schools would be cut in half, from a dollar and a half to seventy-five cents. The students also would be given preference for the first eight thousand seats sold.

The Garden already had been turned into an armed camp. The police responded in customary fashion. Commissioner Thomas F. Murphy ordered the Garden patrolled, with the intent of keeping out gamblers and bookmakers. Assistant Chief Inspector James R. Kennedy stationed thirty plainclothesmen at strategic points in and around the arena for the fight between Tony Janiro and Fritzie Pruden. Presumably, they would inquire of each patron whether he had wagered anything on the fight. Predictably, no one was arrested and no one was turned away. Bookmakers throughout the city reported no decline in business. The number of bettors was undiminished, and the total betting handle was about the same. The only difference was that it had become difficult to get down a bet of more than five thousand dollars on a single game.

That was the extent of it. The gambling would continue as it always had, because people chose to gamble. The police could not keep anyone with the price of a ticket out of the Garden, and it would have mattered little if they could. Bookmakers had never been inclined to solicit bets from strangers in a public arena. Perhaps the fatal flaw of police mentality is a naïveté with regard to the intelligence of any but their own. The truth was that a bookmaker could often spot a cop much more quickly than a cop would know a bookmaker, and the bookmaker did not have to concern himself with the burden of proof.

So the police would conduct their patrols, the NCAA would offer resolutions, the colleges would issue rulings, and legislatures would pass new laws. Institutions can be trusted never to act counter to their natures. But none of it mattered now. Nothing could be changed. The only ones to be hurt by the new regulations would be those players who were not involved; those who would be driven from the city in search of scholarships in the South or the Midwest, and those who remained but who would never have the opportunity to play ball in the Garden.

The despair of it all was summed up by Hal Uplinger, who had come from the West Coast to play for LIU. "One day," he said, "you're playing for the best team in the country, and the next day you're part of nothing."

11

The "key figure" from Florida turned out to be Lou Lipman, LIU's high scorer from the teams of 1947–48 and 1948–49. Lipman, who was arrested at his home in Hollywood, Florida, on March 2, was charged with throwing only one game, for which he received the sum of three hundred dollars. These were not very imposing numbers for so key a figure, but then Lipman had a story to tell. It was a story of threats, intimidation, double crosses, and deceit, and it fired a path that led to other players, and a second major fixer who had preceded Sollazzo onto the scene.

Lipman told the district attorney that he first suspected something was amiss after a game with Southern California during the 1947–48 season when a teammate half jokingly told him, "Lou, if you'd made one more basket you'd have gotten us all shot." During that same season he discussed his suspicions with another player and was told that if he was not careful he would be "tied in a sack and dumped in the river." That summer, while playing at a Catskill Mountain resort, Lipman was invited into the deal by Eddie Gard, Natie Miller, and a player not yet arrested, whom Lipman called Mr. X. Gard told him they could split seven thousand five hundred dollars among them if Lipman would "go along." Lipman rejected that offer and two subsequent offers before arrangements were made for the fixing of the LIU–Duquesne game at the Garden on New Year's Day 1949. Lipman apparently agreed to accept eleven hundred dollars as his share of a five-thousand-dollar package to keep the score of the game below the four-and-a-half-point spread. Hogan said the fixer went to the LIU locker room before the game to notify the players that the deal was on. Lipman contended that he did not know about it until a time-out during the game when Miller told him, "We're in on this one." He also said that he did not know that he was being paid to throw the game. He thought it was a "come-on bonus," he said, "to get me used to money."

LIU lost the game 64–55, and the resulting payoff did not serve to accustom Lipman to the feel of money because he never got his eleven hundred dollars. A few days after the game, Lipman, Miller, and X met Gard near the campus, but Gard said he did not have the money. The next night Miller and Lipman went to Gard's home to meet with a former player, identified as Y, who was supposed to have paid the money to Gard. Mr. X was not present. He was to be dealt a short hand and given only six hundred dollars for his efforts. However, when Y arrived, he said he did not bring the money with him. He said the fixer was holding it and that it would be tripled on the next fixed game. Lipman reneged. He said he wanted out. Lipman told the DA that he was involved in no subsequent fixes, but that on its next road trip LIU lost four straight games under "suspicious circumstances."

After attending summer session in 1949, Lipman again sought out Mr. Y, who told him that the money had been returned to the fixer. Lipman looked up the fixer and was told that Y was lying. Lipman relayed the information to Gard and Miller, and then met with Y in the lobby of a midtown hotel. Y gave him an envelope containing one thousand dollars and told him to give it to Gard to be split up. Lipman was given three hundred dollars, and the payment was made more than six months after the fixed game. It was said to be all the money he ever received. Yet he was described as a key figure in the scandal. It was not an overstatement, for Lipman's testimony led, more than a month later, to the arrest of X and Y.

X was Dick Feurtado, a teammate of Lipman's who was brought East from Santa Cruz, California, where he worked as a gas-station attendant. Feurtado admitted receiving four thousand dollars for his part in fixing the games with North Carolina State, Cincinnati, and Syracuse in 1949–50, as well as the Duquesne game the previous season. Feurtado, it turned out, made out better than Lipman on the Duquesne game. Although he was dealt out of the fix money divided by Gard, Miller, and Lipman, it was discovered that he received, as promised, one thousand dollars from Sollazzo for fixing the same game.

Y was a somewhat better known personality and far more of a "key figure" than either Feurtado or Lipman. The police had been seeking Jackie Goldsmith since the scandal broke, on February 18. He had disappeared from his Brooklyn home immediately after the arrest of Gard and Sollazzo, and he was picked up more than two months later while leaving a dry-cleaning store in Brooklyn. He had made some preparations for the day of his arrest. Assistant District Attorney Vincent A. G. O'Connor, who was leading the investigation, said Goldsmith had torn parts of pages from his address book, and he persistently refused to divulge names or details of games to the district attorney. Goldsmith pleaded not guilty, insisted on his innocence, and contended throughout the investigation that he knew nothing about the fixing of basketball games.

He was the first former player who flatly and consistently refused to cooperate. Of course, Goldsmith had the least to gain and the most to lose by making any admissions. His roots to the underworld ran deep, and they were not of recent vintage. He was not, like Gard, simply a contact and a runner for those more highly placed. Goldsmith had come a long way since his sophomore year at LIU in 1945. He had scratched his way to the top of his trade, high enough for the DA to describe him as a "master fixer." According to O'Connor and Assistant District Attorney Morris Goldman, Goldsmith gave no names, offered no information, and answered no questions. The code of silence is the glue of the underworld. It is as highly prized in the back streets of Brooklyn as it is in the secret councils of government and the highest echelons of the military, and it is more often adhered to. It is not mere chance that decades later the link between the CIA and the Mafia would be revealed, not by the Mafia, but by agents of the CIA. The underworld has always exercised the greatest discretion in choosing its people.

Goldsmith had had an early start. He was reputed to have been involved in the rigging of games since his sophomore year, when he set a single-season scoring record at LIU with 395 points. He was known then as the Brownsville Bomber, a diminutive five-foot-seven backcourt man who could hit the mark with some consistency from as far as forty-five feet and who, for the two seasons he played, was perhaps the best two-hand set shot ever to appear in the Garden. Goldsmith did not play during his senior year. The rumors of his keeping "bad company" already had traveled some distance, and he chose to sit it out. Even during the two seasons he played, Goldsmith was the subject of much speculation in gambling precincts around the city. Despite his prolific point making, his performances ran hot and cold, and appeared to be tailored very often to the fluctuations of the point spread. He was said to have become, in the past six years, an "intimate of thugs and crooked gamblers." O'Connor charged that Goldsmith was "responsible for the corruption of more college basketball players than any other single person." In the rhetoric of overstatement that was so much a part of the early fifties, O'Connor noted, "In Goldsmith we see all the phases of corruption exemplified. He is the sum of all that is wrong in the basketball picture in recent years."

The only charge brought against Goldsmith was the bribing of Gard, Lipman, Feurtado, and Miller to fix the LIU–Duquesne game. Yet bail was set at fifty thousand dollars, half of what O'Connor requested. O'Connor said his request for high bail was based largely on his concern for Goldsmith's safety. "The people associated with him know what he can give us," O'Connor said. He called Goldsmith an "essential key" to the inquiry because his underworld associations through the years had involved him with several groups of fixers. If Goldsmith was a key to the investigation, it is not likely that he opened many doors. There is no evidence that he ever supplied any information, and certainly his treatment in the courts would indicate a failure to cooperate. As the investigation proceeded and the scandal spread, Goldsmith's bail was lifted, and he was jailed awaiting his sentence, which turned out to be a rather stiff term of two and a half to five years in the state penitentiary.

Indicted with Goldsmith was William Rivlin, a small-time gambler who had served a year in 1949 for his part in the attempt to fix the George Washington–Manhattan game, which was played three days after LIU–Duquesne. Rivlin was said to have been involved with Goldsmith in making bribe offers to the four LIU players, but it could not be immediately verified, for Rivlin was nowhere to be found. He was indicted in absentia, and a fourteen-state alarm was issued for his arrest.

During a three-week period in March, barely a month since the City and LIU scandals came to public notice, a scattering of small-time gamblers was picked up from one end of the country to the other. They were, for the most part, the little men who worked at the fringes of their trade—contacts, runners, bag men, penny-ante gamblers hot for a quick score—whose lines to the top were barely visible.

One of the least imposing of these figures was Albert R. Scroggins, an ex-convict who had served six months on a robbery charge in Birmingham, Alabama. Scroggins was charged with offering Ken Flower, a nineteen-year-old sophomore forward at the University of Southern California, fifteen hundred dollars to dump a game with UCLA. Flower reported the incident to his coach, whose name, ironically enough, was Forrest Twogood. Scroggins had told Flower that his team, which was the underdog, would lose anyway, "so you might as well lose by twelve and make some money." Coach Twogood knew how to use such ammunition. He told his team about the attempted fix in a locker room meeting before the game, and Southern Cal went out to upset UCLA 43–41 and gain a tie for first place in the Southern Division of the Pacific Coast League. Scroggins, who was picked up in his hotel room while the game was in progress, appeared to have very few connections. He was indicted for attempted bribery and jailed in default of bail. He pleaded innocent by reason of insanity and was examined by three court-appointed psychiatrists. He was found to be less insane than he had hoped and was fined $3,500, a sum he was unable to raise. He worked off the fine in the local jail at the rate of ten dollars a day.

Of more significance was the release, on thirty-five thousand dollars' bail, of Robert Sabatini, who had been held since February 18 as a material witness. Sabatini was an associate and neighbor of Salvatore Sollazzo, and it can be inferred that such information as he possessed was now the property of the district attorney's office. The case against Sollazzo was building, and it was moving in more than one direction.

Shortly after his arrest, the books of his jewelry manufacturing firm were seized, and on February 28 Sollazzo was indicted by a federal grand jury on charges of income-tax evasion. Since Sollazzo was then under the criminal jurisdiction of New York City, his arraignment on the income-tax charge required an agreement between District Attorney Hogan and a U.S. attorney by the name of Irving Saypol. Saypol had other things on his mind at the time. A week later he would begin presenting the people's case against Julius and Ethel Rosenberg and Morton Sobell, who were accused of giving atomic secrets to the Soviet Union. But if the case against Sollazzo was being pressed by a formidable pair of prosecutors, it cannot be said that his own counsel was entirely overmatched. For he was being represented by William W. Kleinman, a former assistant district attorney for Kings County, who was perhaps better known as the attorney for Louis (Lepke) Buchalter, the onetime associate of such as Albert Anastasia and Lucky Luciano, who had gone to the electric chair on a murder charge in 1945.

The federal charge did not in any way interfere with local proceedings. One week later, a New York grand jury handed up a thirteen-count bribery indictment against Sollazzo which carried a maximum penalty of sixty-five years in prison and a total of one hundred thirty thousand dollars in fines. At the same time, the Department of Justice had moved to deport Sollazzo on grounds of moral turpitude, entering the country without a visa, and misrepresenting himself as a U.S. citizen to immigration authorities. He continued to be held without bail on the recommendation of the district attorney, who said his life might be in danger if he were released. At his arraignment, DA O'Connor described Sollazzo as an intimate of the "notorious underworld figures, Salvatore and Willie Moretti and Salvatore Spitale," who reputedly were members of the mob run by Joe Adonis. He already had been linked, at least inferentially, to Frank Erickson, Meyer Lansky, Lucky Luciano, and Frank Costello.

Costello was the acknowledged high prince of the New York underworld at the time. The heft and breadth of his power was, in fact, being sketched in detail before the entire country just three days after Sollazzo's arraignment. For Costello was the central figure as a Senate Crime Investigating Committee, chaired by Senator Estes Kefauver, opened televised hearings into organized crime in New York's Foley Square courthouse on March 12. Together with Joe Adonis, Costello was said to be the leader of one of the nation's two major crime syndicates, whose territorial axis ran down the east coast from New York to Miami. He had climbed the ladder as a smart and aggressive bootlegger during Prohibition, and when the market moved he moved with it. The engines that powered the machine of organized crime in the early fifties were not yet fueled by drugs; the big stake was gambling. The Kefauver Committee estimated that twenty billion dollars in illegal gambling receipts changed hands in 1950, and Frank Costello had his finger on all the right levers.

On the very first day of the hearings, testimony was offered that Costello had been paid sixty thousand dollars by George Morton Levy, head of Roosevelt Raceway, to keep bookmakers away from the track. A racetrack is fertile ground for a bookmaker. The pari-mutuel windows may be adequate for the taste of a two-dollar bettor, but a man who wishes to bet a thousand dollars on a race is likely to give preference to a more rarefied business climate. He has no desire to see his wager calculated into the track odds. A bet of a thousand dollars on a six-to-one horse could drop the odds suddenly and substantially. It is also ice cream and cake to the tote-board watchers, the small bettors who are waiting for the opportunity to get down with the smart money. They will watch the board for a horse that attracts a sudden influx of betting capital and then bet the horse themselves, dropping the odds even further. A large bet placed with an entrepreneur will keep the bet off the board and, no less important, escape the notice of the Internal Revenue Service should the horse win. So bookmakers have been known to flourish at the racetrack, much to the peril of the track's operator, for the presence of bookmakers was sufficient grounds for the revocation of his license. Frank Costello, apparently, knew how to keep a racetrack clean, and he understood the value of such security.

Costello became something of an instant television celebrity. He had, right at the outset, objected to being shown on camera. He said it violated the privacy of his relations with his counsel. And so all through the long hours of his testimony, the television audience listened to a disembodied voice while it watched, on flickering black-and-white screens, a modern ballet of the hands. Costello's hands occupied the center of the screen, twisting to the rhythm of the questions put to him, coiling a crumpled handkerchief, rubbing his palms together, rolling a small ball of paper between thumb and forefinger. Costello denied having any connections with bookmaking, but he admitted accepting the sixty-thousand-dollar fee to pass the word that there would be no bookmaking at Roosevelt Raceway. Was that not an excessive sum to pay a man who had so few connections? he was asked. No more excessive, he replied, than fees charged by attorneys for their own services. But the procedure was, in effect, just that simple. Costello passed the word, and the bookmakers kept their business clear of the track.

The connection between Costello and Sollazzo was never firmly established. One might believe, if he chose, that they resided in the same apartment building merely by chance, and that Costello, who after all had admitted to having some small influence among the betting establishment, was unaware that he had as a neighbor a man given to betting as much as thirty thousand dollars on a basketball game. The greater likelihood was, of course, that Sollazzo moved in some very tight circles.

In the end, Costello told the committee little it did not already know. Three days after the hearings began, he declined to answer any more questions and invited a contempt citation by walking out of the room, saying that his health was impaired. His health must indeed have been poor, for rather than return to the hearing room, he sat by while he was cited for contempt, convicted, and sentenced to eighteen months in Lewisburg Federal Penitentiary.

What the committee was to learn about gambling would come two weeks later from a "retired" professional gambler named Sidney A. Brodson. Brodson, who came from Milwaukee, was not your everyday bettor. He was a graduate of the universities of Illinois and Wisconsin, he held a law degree, and he was licensed to practice in both states. He had practiced law for a short time, he told the committee, but he found the going to be tough during the Depression. He needed a new source of income. He had always been interested in sports, and he was a casual but unusually successful bettor. If he studied the teams closely, he found, he could beat the point spread on college basketball games with a degree of regularity. Brodson decided to make a career of betting on basketball.

He won with such consistency that he found it necessary to spread his bets across the country to keep from affecting the odds on a game. A wager of two thousand dollars, which was his average bet, was often enough to influence the point spread among Milwaukee bookmakers. Brodson chose instead to parcel out his wagers with bookmakers in other cities. He did not deal directly with the bookmakers. His out-of-town bets were placed by his own representatives, known in the trade as "beards." The beards were paid nothing. They found their compensation in knowing which way to bet a game, and that arrangement appeared to keep them content. Brodson was asked how he knew that beards from all over the country would pay off on a winning bet. His answer was direct, and it cut to the bone. A professional gambler, he said, had no stock in trade except his reputation. When it is gone, he is bankrupt. One hundred professional gamblers, he told the committee and the nation, constitute a better credit risk than one hundred reputable businessmen.

Inevitably, Brodson was questioned about the point-shaving scandal, which was then breaking into its second month. He told the committee that he had no direct knowledge of specifically rigged games, but that every professional gambler in the country had suspected that games in Madison Square Garden were being tampered with for years. He wagered as much as one million dollars a year on college basketball, he said, but he had not bet on a Garden game in three years. It was during the 1947–48 season that he began to notice strange results and abnormal betting patterns. The odds would fluctuate too rapidly shortly before a game. He watched the point spreads very closely in every part of the country, he noted. He even retained a full-time employee who received 15 percent of the profits in return for reading one hundred sports pages a day and supplying Brodson with the information he needed.

Since Brodson's betting business had relied so heavily on interstate transactions, one of the committee members, Senator Alexander Wiley, a Wisconsin Republican, wondered whether federal legislation might not be effective in stemming the trade. How, he asked Brodson, would professional gamblers circumvent a federal law prohibiting the transmission of wagers by telephone, telegraph, or radio across state lines?

"Give me thirty minutes to think it over," Brodson replied. "I guarantee they will find a way."

The Kefauver Committee had its run. The televised hearings, which lasted eight days, earned the senator a vice-presidential nomination in 1952, sent Frank Costello to jail, and drove a former New York City mayor, William O'Dwyer, into exile in Mexico, where he was serving as U.S. ambassador. Its television ratings were excellent. Nielsen estimated that twice as many people watched the hearings as viewed the World Series the previous fall. It should not have come as a very great surprise, for the hearings fed America's insatiable appetite for revelation and its adolescent curiosity with regard to celebrities.

Indeed, that appetite was being well fed in the early fifties. When the Kefauver Committee folded its tent and moved from Foley Square to Washington, it found it was not the only show in town. The House Committee on Un-American Activities had revived its hearings on Communists in Hollywood. Such personalities as John Garfield, Jose Ferrer, Abe Burrows, and Larry Parks were lifted right off the screen of the Bijou and marched into a congressional hearing room to audition before HUAC. It had been almost four years since HUAC had pilloried the Hollywood Ten—the Unfriendly Ten they were called then—and another pre-election year doubtless seemed a suitable time for a rerun. It was after all in the best Hollywood tradition. The original had been an unqualified success. Political careers were launched from the very bones of ruined film careers, the blacklist had become the equivalent of a constitutional amendment, and the tissue had been peeled from every fear that clogged the drains of the American psyche.

Now the cast of characters was juggled, the script was rewritten, and the sequel was staged as a million-dollar extravaganza, a spectacle larger than life—great names in cameo parts, brief walk-ons by lesser-known personalities, a star-studded cast on a giant screen, and if one kept his eye close to the keyhole he could watch the rushes and see the cuts.

"Are you now or have you ever been . . . ?" they were asked. They demurred, most of them, they cowered, they scratched and shuffled to save their careers. John Garfield, prototype of the tenement street tough, first denied having had any contact with Communists, and finally made his separate peace. He had never joined the Party, he said, but he had on occasion shown unwitting sympathy for the cause. He was a Communist dupe. Some months later, Garfield, swaggering native of New York's East Side, the middleweight champion of *Body and Soul* who refused to take a dive for gamblers (What can you do, kill me? Everybody dies), was preparing an article for *Look* magazine entitled "I Was a Sucker for a Left Hook."

But Larry Parks, who had come to the threshold of stardom playing the title role in *The Jolson Story*, was the first to crack. Parks admitted that, yes, he had been a Communist, from 1941 to 1945, and once the admission was made the meat was in the grinder. Parks was questioned relentlessly, and after several days he began to name names. Three weeks later, Richard Collins, a screen writer, really threw open the gates. He tossed names to the committee like beef to a hound; more than twenty in all, including such as Budd Schulberg, Ring Lardner, Jr., and Robert Rossen. After the hearings, Parks said he had been "forced to crawl through the mud." The irony was that he salvaged nothing. Parks's career was, for the most part, finished. So was Garfield's. In little more than a year, he was dead of a heart attack. For it did not matter what one told the committee. If he admitted Communist affiliation, he was a traitor. If he denied it, he was a dupe or a liar. The fact of being summoned was evidence enough. No formal charges had to be brought, no conviction was necessary, a trial was superfluous. The sentence was always implicit; one simply ceased to work.

The American public did not care to watch former Communists mouth the words of Al Jolson. Certainly they would not send their children. Who could tell what subliminal messages might be woven into the fabric of a tune? Just a year earlier, hadn't Ingrid Bergman's films been banned and boycotted because she had a child out of wedlock? And what was that on the scale of sin when compared with being a Com-you-nist? At least pregnancy was not contagious. But Com-you-nism! Everyone knew it was as invisible and as deadly as nerve gas. Imagine sending your child to the movies on Saturday afternoon and having him return a Com-you-nist after watching Larry Parks play Al Jolson. Poor Larry Parks! Twenty years later he probably would have been boycotted as a racist for singing "Mammy" in blackface.

The Hollywood hearings were little more than a prelude to what was to come. A wave of social paranoia would soon be loosed that would warp the foundation of every institution in America. It started at the top, in the very highest precincts of government, and it filtered down, seeping through every crack in the superstructure, until no part of the nation's life was left untouched.

In May, a nationwide survey reported finding a "subtle, creeping paralysis of thought and speech" on college campuses. It was a precocious study for 1951, more a forecast than a conclusion, for the generation of the fifties would later be known as the Silent Generation. It was as if every college was its own small town, living in the private rhythm of its seasons, immune to the throbbing waters that beat at its walls. There was a war being fought halfway across the globe, a sullen war being waged in an obscure land in the interest of a cause that was nearly impossible to comprehend. It was not at all like World War II; it touched only those who got trapped in it. If one was on a college campus then, it was possible to live through the entire conflict without ever knowing anyone who saw combat. One's brother was not summoned, nor one's friends or neighbors or the delivery boy who brought the groceries on Friday afternoon. It was the first of America's mini-wars, fought by the disadvantaged few, hundreds of thousands of fighting troops skimmed from the scrap heap and sent off to die by a country that gave academic asylum to its privileged and chosen. It was not so much professional ambition that sparked the quest for grades in the early fifties as it was the knowledge that academic standing offered refuge from the draft.

One was grateful. He would not be sent to war. He would not be driven from his home, as perhaps his parents had been. He would be permitted to remain in college and receive a degree, and if it was a New York City college he was attending, his tuition would be paid and even his books would be provided at no cost. What could one think to protest in such a country? Did the Communists have it so good? And so the Silent Generation emerged from the humble gratitude of its forebears.

Of course, the Silent Generation did not think of itself as being silent at all. But then no generation ever comes to know itself until judgment is finally passed by the next. It is possible that there is a rhythm to the turn of generations, a dialectic which insists that the first must create a dream, the second strive for it, and the third try to rewrite it. Your own was caught in the crosswinds of transition. Legatees of Depression and children of war, you would reach adolescence before you would begin to understand that life was not always lived in an atmosphere of crisis. The fifties was the first time in perhaps two decades that one could grow up believing he knew what might be required of him, that if life was hard its rules at least were simple, and if the first imperative was to learn to survive, the second was to be able to survive without working quite so hard at it. And so the sullen mood of estrangement, which turned the engines of the sixties, was hardly to be found on college campuses a decade earlier. Social conscience rarely stretched beyond the streets of one's own neighborhood, and what little political activity was to be found was as brief as the seasons and as bland as a faculty tea. Even student activists, for the most part, were scholarly and sedate, and devoted mainly to no cause more subversive than the election of Adlai Stevenson.

It all seemed rather vapid to you, connected to no reality that might offer the prospect of results. Your own taste had always been for something more immediate, something that gave form and definition to a part of your life. At the end of each day you wanted to be able to count up the pieces, to separate gold from sand, and perhaps begin to divine some notion of how much had finally been won or lost. You could not see how a student rally would help to elect Adlai Stevenson or what compelling change his election might make in your life. Stevenson of Illinois against Eisenhower of Abilene, Kansas, gave no trigger to inspiration that fall; not when the Yankees of the Bronx were playing the Dodgers of Brooklyn in the World Series.

Your own political involvement, such as it was, would not begin for another decade, not until the early sixties when, sitting in a barber's chair, you heard John F. Kennedy speak of a torch being passed to a new generation. Here, at last, was a President with whom you could identify, a hero, an athlete of sorts, a man whose very style one could appropriate, could shape and mold to fit the pattern of one's own life. Kennedy, standing coatless in the January cold, his fingers toying with the button on his suit coat, his hair tossed and parted by the wind, issuing a call to the future that you could believe only because you wanted to believe it. Kennedy, whose speech flowed out on big-city accents; Kennedy, whose ambitions, though hardly immodest, were at least flavored with a sense of irony and wit; Kennedy, with the twitting boyish charm of a good poolroom hustler, whose word was not necessarily truer than the next man's, but whose mood you felt you could read. For there was about him the touch of the familiar, as though you had known men who shared the same field of battle.

But that was 1961, and a new generation had already begun to set roots in the quickened conscience of America. The country had changed vastly in the past ten years, and the shift was perhaps most discernible on college campuses, where only a decade earlier the search for Communists had stirred little sentiment. Even when Dr. V. Jerauld McGill was dismissed from the faculty of Hunter College it did not seem to be a matter of great concern either to his students or to his associates. McGill, who was a professor of philosophy, was abruptly severed from the faculty along with two of his colleagues— Dr. Louis Weisner, of the mathematics department, and Dr. Charles W. Hughes, who taught music. Each had spent more than a quarter century at Hunter, and each had admitted to holding brief memberships in the Communist Party in the late thirties and forties. The trio was questioned at length by the Senate Investigating Committee in 1952, and the committee concluded that their presence on the faculty was a clear indication of "Communist infiltration" of college campuses. The committee somehow failed to note that all three had "infiltrated" the campus long before they had become Communists and continued to teach after they had renounced their memberships. McGill joined the Hunter faculty in 1929 and did not affiliate with the Communist Party until 1936. Weisner and Hughes came to Hunter in 1927 and joined the Party eleven years later. Still, the three cases were cited as "clinical demonstrations that Communists and the Communist Party are . . . the deadly enemy of academic freedom."

One had spent a semester with Dr. McGill, and it was difficult to envision him an agent of Moscow. He was a tall, spindly man of middle years, with a graying head, a brief mustache, and an addiction to a well-worn pipe. He did not appear a likely candidate for enemy infiltration, and a single week in his class might have served to dispel all suspicions. If McGill was guilty of any offense in the classroom, it was a deadening monotone and an inclination toward the banal. Each day he read laboriously from the works of Plato or Aristotle or Berkeley, grinding his way through fifty minutes' worth of text, from bell to bell. It was not even Plato's *Republic*, which was at least a quasi-political discursion, that he assigned, but the *Symposium*, a dialogue devoted to the nature of love. Not a single political fillip dropped from McGill's lips that semester, not the first suggestion of a controversial or contentious remark in a subject area that might be considered meat and potatoes for political indoctrination. One could only wonder at what of a subversive nature might have worked its way into the curriculum in the departments of mathematics and music.

Nonetheless, the Senate Investigating Committee was convinced that freedom of thought was imperiled by their presence on a college campus, and they were summarily dismissed as a means of "protecting academic freedom from such enslavements." Their true transgression, it should be noted, was that they did not cooperate with the committee. Unlike so many of their Hollywood counterparts, they would not serve up the names of their colleagues. McGill, to his credit, taught his finest lesson in philosophy outside the classroom. He drank the hemlock. So he and the others, the great enslavers, were banished from their profession, and not a voice was raised or a word spoken in their behalf. There were no rallies, no protests, no questions asked by faculty or students. They were gone, and that was all.

One should not have been surprised at the silence. A few years earlier, on the same campus, one had circulated a petition asking administrative clemency for the fixed basketball players. It was not a very radical document. It requested only that the players be reinstated and permitted to continue their studies pending the outcome of litigation. It was a position not without sympathy among the student body, but there were few who would sign their names to the petition. Petitions were used as weapons in the fifties. They were resurrected years after their signing, often as proof of allegiance to a cause that had since lost favor. People paid with their jobs and reputations for signing petitions that had seemed harmless twenty years earlier. No, they would not put their names to it, and it was not likely that it would have mattered if they did.

The case had already been fed into the judicial machinery, and no college administration could be expected to act on its own until it had been disposed of in the courts. Indeed, it was not possible to know what might yet bubble to the surface. In the two weeks following the arrest of the first City College players, a total of eleven players and former players had been arrested and booked. The scandal had been spreading in many directions, but no one expected it to turn full circle, back to City College and its grand-slam team. But on March 27, the remaining key players from the double-championship team—Irwin Dambrot, Norm Mager, and Herb Cohen—admitted taking bribes to fix three games during the grand-slam season. Also implicated in the manipulation of those games were Ed Roman and Al Roth, whose earlier admissions had covered only three games played the following season, 1950–51. It turned out then that the City team—or at least five of its members—had been dumping right from the start, for the first fixed game was against Southern Methodist on December 8, 1949, only the second varsity game that the sophomores—Roman, Roth, and Cohen—played in Madison Square Garden. Ed Warner and Floyd Layne were not involved in the fixes during the 1949–50 season. In all probability, Roman, Roth, and Mager were recruited the previous summer, when they played for the same resort-hotel team in the Catskill Mountains. Warner had spent that summer working in the stockroom of a dress company, and Layne was employed in an auto-parts factory.

At the time of their arrest, Dambrot was a student at Columbia Dental School, Mager was playing professionally for the Baltimore Bullets of the NBA, and Cohen was completing his junior year at City. It might have been nothing more than coincidence, but three days earlier, Don Forman, a star for NYU in the mid-forties, was charged with having approached several City College players for a gambler other than Salvatore Sollazzo. Forman, a five-foot-ten-inch guard, had played in three National Invitation Tournaments for NYU between 1944 and 1948, and had scored as many as thirty-eight points in a game against Duke University in 1948. Forman was brought to New York from Jacksonville, Florida, where he and his father were conducting a liquor business. Forman was said to have completed none of his fix attempts, and the City players he had contacted were not named. He was released in five thousand dollars' bail as a material witness.

Dambrot, Mager, and Cohen were set free on bail of one thousand dollars each, after admitting holding down the points in the games against SMU, UCLA, and Niagara. Roman, Roth, Dambrot, and Mager had been promised one thousand dollars apiece, and Cohen five hundred dollars, to keep the spread below seven in the SMU game. However, SMU performed so poorly that City, even playing in ragtag fashion, won by fourteen points and covered the spread. The players, of course, did not receive their money, but they did collect, at the same rate, on December 27, when City, favored over UCLA, lost the game 60–53. Roman, curiously enough, was the game's high scorer with twenty-two points. It was City's second loss of the season, and it occurred as part of a doubleheader in which St. John's defeated Utah for its eleventh straight victory. After the UCLA game, Holman was vehement in his criticism of Roman, Warner, and Dambrot. He accused them of "playing stupidly" and called Roman's defense against Carl Kraushaar "inexcusable." He also noted that Dambrot had thrown a number of wild passes while scoring only a single basket. The entire team made only 25 percent of its shots from the floor, and Holman said he could not see his team beating St. John's in their game the following week. City, of course, played its best game of the season in defeating St. John's and embarking on a seven-game winning streak.

With the team riding its crest, Roman and Dambrot decided they had had enough of their dealings with gamblers and would take part in no further arrangements. That left only Mager, who was the contact man, Roth, and Cohen to guarantee the points against Niagara on February 16. The gamblers, who had not been named by the district attorney's office, could hardly feel they had a sure thing when two of the three fixed players were not even starters. They sweetened the pot, doubling Cohen's share to one thousand dollars, and promising Mager and Roth bonuses of two hundred fifty dollars if they were successful. Niagara, as it turned out, ran City into the boards and won the game 68–61.

"We may be going sour," Holman said after the game. "They're making too many mistakes, throwing the ball away and—well, just sloppy."

The Niagara game did in fact begin a skid that dropped the Beavers out of the national ratings for the duration of the season. They did not regain their equilibrium until they rallied for season-ending victories against Manhattan and NYU. The five players were said to have turned down a substantial offer to fix their opening-round game in the NIT against San Francisco, and there apparently were no other rigged games during the 1949–50 season.

The new arrests obliged the district attorney's office to widen its investigation. Sollazzo and his agents were in no way involved in the fixes that took place during the grand-slam season. In effect, two separate betting scandals had taken root in New York in consecutive years. Some players had taken part in both, but the gambling interests were as distinct from one another as competing corporations in private industry. Betting syndicates adhered to the free enterprise system as devoutly as the biggest and best of America's conglomerates. Shortly after questioning Mager, Dambrot, and Cohen, Hogan announced that he was seeking a number of other fixers along the eastern seacoast. He did not identify them, but he said he knew who they were, and some of them were being tracked among the winter resorts in Florida.

One month later, Eli Klukofsky, better known as Eli Kaye, was arrested outside a Miami nightclub and charged with bribing the City players to throw the three games in 1949–50. Kaye, twenty-nine years old and a former shipyard welder, admitted paying Mager a total of eight thousand dollars to be distributed among himself, Roman, Roth, Dambrot, and Cohen.

Hogan promised new arrests and said the scandal would continue to spread. He estimated that fixers bearing no connection to Sollazzo —Kaye included—had set up betting coups on at least twenty Madison Square Garden games dating back to December 1948. Since Sollazzo and his group were known to have fixed at least eight games, the total would very likely exceed thirty over a three-year period. It was not an insignificant number. It meant that anyone who had paid his way into the Garden for a college doubleheader during each of those three seasons had, in all probability, seen a fixed basketball game. And, as it turned out, Hogan's figures were found to be conservative.

13

By the end of March, seventeen New York City college basketball players—including Poppe and Byrnes of Manhattan—had been arrested. The arrests of Feurtado and Goldsmith three weeks later, brought the total to nineteen players from four colleges, and involved the fixing of at least twenty-three games. Four of the five colleges in New York that played some portion of their home schedules at Madison Square Garden—Manhattan, City, LIU, and NYU—had been implicated in the scandal. Only St. John's had escaped unscathed. The only mention of a St. John's player being so much as approached by a gambler came on March 9, when Bob (Zeke) Zawoluk disclosed that Sollazzo had offered him a "present" if he helped run up a big score against City on January 2, 1951. Zawoluk said he ignored the remark and never heard from Sollazzo again. The offer, he said, was made to him two nights before the game at a New Year's Eve party Sollazzo had held in the Latin Quarter, a well-known and elegant night spot in midtown Manhattan. Zawoluk, and perhaps a dozen other players, had been invited to the party by Eddie Gard. Most of the players were already doing business with Sollazzo and Gard, and the party apparently was one of their fringe benefits.

Sollazzo's offer to Zawoluk was a curious one. Four of the City players—Roman, Roth, Warner, and Layne—had admitted receiving bonuses of two hundred fifty dollars apiece from Sollazzo as a reward for staying within three points of St. John's and beating the nine-point spread by which the Redmen were favored. If Sollazzo had indeed offered Zawoluk a "present" to run up a big score against City, he certainly would not have contracted to pay four City players one thousand dollars to do the same against St. John's. One possible explanation is that Sollazzo first approached Zawoluk, but when the St. John's center ignored him, he decided to go the other way and bet a City College upset. It is not the likeliest explanation, for one would have to assume that less than forty-eight hours before the game Sollazzo still had not decided which team he was going to back. Further, if Sollazzo wished to bet on St. John's, the favorite, why had he not asked the City players to assure that St. John's exceeded the spread? He had been doing business with them for almost a month. Just three days earlier, on December 28, they had fixed the score of their game with Arizona. It obviously would be easier for them to hold the score down than it would be for Zawoluk to roll it up. Instead of taking that almost certain route, Sollazzo, the "sure thing" gambler, is said to have approached a player on the opposing team for the first time, at a New Year's Eve party two nights before the game, and offered him a "present" to help beat a team that had dumped for him twice within the past month. Then, rebuffed, he chose to switch his backing from the favorite to the underdog, hoping that bonus money would provide motivation for the City team to upset the spread.

It is, of course, a possibility, but it is not necessarily the first scenario that would come to mind. The greater likelihood is that Sollazzo had already decided to bet on City. He was, after all, one of the very few who knew that the Beavers were better than their record indicated. Two of their three losses had been prearranged, and their five-and-three record going into the St. John's game could just as easily have been seven and one. They were not, Sollazzo might have figured, a legitimate nine-point underdog; not if they were playing at the peak of their game. So given the inflated point spread

—the sweetest of sweets to a gambler—Sollazzo elects to go with the underdog and nourishes the players' incentive by the offer of cash bonuses. Then, with Zawoluk a guest at his party, he thinks to insure his bet further by asking the St. John's center *not* to run up a big score against City. A below-par performance by the opposition's high scorer would be double insurance against St. John's winning by more than nine points. But Zawoluk, indifferent to the proposal in any event, might well have misunderstood Sollazzo's intent.

In fact, Sollazzo's casual offer to Zawoluk was the only firsthand evidence of any approach made to a St. John's player. None was ever arrested, and none ever reported an attempt more concrete than the one made to Zawoluk. At one juncture, there was word that Zawoluk and a teammate, Jack McMahon, were questioned at Hogan's office and released, but even that was difficult to verify, and that was the extent of it. St. John's was the only one of the five schools to remain unsullied. One could not know for certain how intently the DA's office pursued its investigation into the possibility of St. John's involvement, or whether its exclusion from so much as a whisper of scandal was thought to be cause for wonder. But on the streets and in the betting parlors there was a bit of speculation.

The word had spread quickly through the neighborhood, just days after the first LIU arrests. It was that St. John's would not be touched, that Madison Avenue had intervened. The reference was not to New York's advertising agencies. In the manicured suburbs of Westchester County, the term Madison Avenue might have called forth the picture of young, lean executives in Brooks Brothers suits and button-down shirts and narrow ties with knots no larger than a thumbnail. But in the streets of the boroughs it meant something quite different. One thought immediately of a moon-faced man in scarlet clerical attire whose residence was the austere, solitary structure on Madison Avenue and Fiftieth Street, the Archdiocese of New York. There were not many men in the city whose power was the equal of Francis Cardinal Spellman's. It was a subtle, silent, almost subliminal power that Spellman wielded, because its source could never be isolated nor its shape given dimension. It bore, curiously enough, some small resemblance to the power of the underworld, where the consequences of noncompliance were implied but never spoken. Frank Costello could clear Roosevelt Raceway of bookmakers simply by passing the word, and Spellman's own persuasiveness, in entirely different quarters, was no less imposing, for there were many who believed that his connections had root in a far loftier domain. His wishes, then, were not to be taken lightly. One does not shoot craps with salvation.

So it is conceivable that the Cardinal might have exercised, if he had chosen, a degree of influence in the district attorney's office. Frank Hogan, whose reputation for being beyond corruption was rarely disputed, nonetheless might not have been altogether immune to promptings from so ethereal a source. On the streets, it was taken on faith that St. John's had been spared by divine intervention. The evidence for such a conclusion was far from compelling. Certainly one possessed no information that might be entertained in the courts. The story had derived from the least authentic but most reliable of sources, the very same sources that had insisted that basketball games were being rigged long before the first arrests were made. A professional gambler, legend has it, knows that a key ball player has sprained an ankle approximately thirty seconds *before* the injury is incurred. One did not ask verification, and only suckers bet against "the word."

The speculation regarding St. John's involvement was more than the fleeting ruminations of street-corner sleuths. The belief that Spellman intervened still endures, and is so widely accepted that the suggestion that St. John's might, in fact, have been clean is taken for naïveté. Sooner express the conviction that Richard Nixon knew nothing of the Watergate break-in.

Junius Kellogg, the Manhattan player who blew the whistle that started the landslide, laughed when the interviewer suggested that St. John's had managed to remain absolutely pure.

"Come on, Stan, you're shittin' me," he said.

The interviewer noted that some people suspected that the Church might have intervened. Kellogg feigned surprise.

"That's very smart," he said.

"You don't want to say anything further about it?" he was asked.

"Nooooo way!" he said. "But I can tell you there were a lot of frightened dudes around then."

Marty Glickman discussed it at somewhat greater length.

"Mine is only conjecture," he said, "the same conjecture that was current then and still exists today—that St. John's had 'divine' protection from the Cardinal on down. I do know that there were some St. John's ball players that were very police-oriented, by which I mean there were many policemen in their families. Maybe it was because of that and the protection of the Church that they were never exposed.

"I can tell you now, so many years later, of an incident on a bus ride back from a St. John's road game. I sat down alongside one of the ball players, and he appeared to be very down, very concerned.

" 'What's the matter?' I asked him.

" 'I'm worried,' he said. 'I just got word that there's a detective waiting for me at the other end.'

" 'I'm sorry to hear that,' I said. 'Have you got something to be worried about?'

"He didn't answer. There was just this wordless pause. Yeah, he was worried. If he were an honest guy he might have been mad. 'What do they want from me?' he would have been thinking. He would have been indignant. But he wasn't. He was just worried, scared. So maybe he was involved. I don't know that. I have nothing specific."

When Glickman speculates on the involvement of St. John's, he does not speak with the voice of cynicism. He was as close to the college basketball scene as any at the time, and yet he admits to being shocked when the scandal broke.

"I never believed it until the confessions were in," he said. "I just couldn't believe that they would do such a thing. Many people told me they were dumping, including ex-ball players who told me that they had dumped. 'Marty,' they would say to me, 'believe me, I know,

I did it, I was a part of it.' But I didn't believe it, I didn't *want* to believe it. And I had very little understanding of *why* they did it. I knew they were poor, but . . . It was sad, it was really sad."

He did not understand why they had done it. They were poor, most of them, they needed the money. But that is a reason, not really an explanation. It explains only why they were ready to dump for relatively small sums. The fact is that very little of the bribe money was spent or invested. Most of it was hidden. After the initial arrests, the district attorney's office calculated that Roman, Roth, Warner, Layne, White, Bigos, and Smith had received a total of $30,250 in bribes. Of that sum, $26,430 was recovered from assorted places of concealment, which meant that only $3,820 had been spent by the seven players. Eighty-seven percent of the money had been stashed for months in flowerpots, attics, clothes linings, and safe-deposit boxes. It had not been used to buy food, clothing, or automobiles. The players' standard of living had not improved noticeably. It is an axiom of sociologists that rich kids do not steal bicycles. Certainly not; they steal cars, and it is not unreasonable to conclude that had the players been closer to financial prosperity only their price would have changed. No, the need for money was not the critical factor. None of the players had about him the mood of a criminal. If they had not been college basketball players, it is not likely they would have ended up in the courts. They would not have stolen the money. They would not have robbed banks or knocked over gas stations or rolled drunks in Central Park. The likelihood is that most of them had committed the one crime for profit of which they were capable.

They had, of course, functioned in an environment in which it might have been more difficult to play it straight than it was to accept a bribe. For point shaving was as much a part of college basketball in the forties and fifties as the two-hand set shot. The player, like NYU's Jim Brasco, who saw the color of the money and turned his head was part of a minority as fragmentary as the cop who declined the favors of the storekeepers on his beat. He would be obliged, furthermore, to undergo the rigors of a basketball season nagged by the suspicion, if not the knowledge, that some of his teammates might be trying to lose games that he was trying to win. It could not be a happy alternative, and even less agreeable was the prospect of reporting the offer and touching off a scandal of sizable proportions.

For those who chose to go along with the deal, there was no shortage of rationalizations. A college athlete works as hard and as long as the most diligent of his professors, his coach, and the administrators who make the rules he must live by, and his only reward is a varsity letter. If he happened to play basketball for City College, he helped to bring more than fifty thousand dollars a year into the school's coffers. Basketball revenues paid the bills for all other intercollegiate sports at City, including football, which lost an estimated sixteen thousand dollars a year. Profits from the games played at Madison Square Garden supported a variety of college activities. They paid the salaries of everyone connected with the games—the coaches, the referees, the ushers, the ticket takers, and the peanut vendors. In fact, everyone shared in those profits except the performers who brought the patrons through the turnstiles. The players, of course, were well aware of just how valuable a property they were. And they knew, too, that the coaches and assistant coaches were no less aware of it, for most of the players had been assiduously recruited.

Roman was already enrolled at the University of Cincinnati when he was persuaded to return home and play for City. The prospect of playing in the 1952 Olympics enticed Warner to switch from LIU even after workouts had begun. And he no doubt left LIU at some sacrifice, because LIU subsidized its athletes more lavishly than most schools in the city. Scholarships included full tuition, free books, and the payment of all fees. There also was reason to believe that the attainment of grades, and therefore eligibility, was not taken very seriously, and that varsity athletes were sometimes privileged to take courses that required less than academic excellence. The athletic departments of all the schools served as employment agencies for the athletes, providing them with summer jobs in the Catskills, and in some instances campus jobs at which they did not always have to work and which paid them bonuses after a particularly distinguished performance on the court. Some players, it would later be discovered, did not even meet the entrance requirements of the schools for which they played. Their transcripts were altered, sometimes drastically, to grant them eligibility. So a varsity player knew that he was special. He knew that he was coveted by the college that recruited him, and that the rules were something to be winked at and adjusted to suit the occasion. He was aware, in effect, that cheating was a part of the game, an indulgence that had the blessing of coaches and the countenance of deans.

It soon became apparent that the betting scandal had grown out of a system that was inherently corrupt. Colleges depended largely on gate receipts for the support of their athletic programs, and so coaches labored under pressure to assemble a team that would attract paying customers. It was necessary, therefore, to win with some consistency, and the coaches responded by seeking out, by recruiting, quality players. An all-city player might know that his skills were up for auction, and if one college was inclined to bend its rules a bit, another might feel the need to scuttle them entirely. Thus an amateur sport acquired the cast of professionalism. The players were treated as professionals in all respects but one: they were not paid for their efforts. And so they followed the example of their elders: they tampered with the rules. If a player could be recruited rather than bought, and subsidized without being paid, then the player, in turn, might feel that he could control the score of a game without really dumping it.

It was a package of circumstances that was gift-wrapped for interpretation by any sound behaviorist. Once the facts were known the problem stated itself: too much emphasis was placed upon winning. It was a convenient notion. Coaches and administrators were ready, some even eager, to plead guilty to a charge of overemphasis. They did not bribe players to play for them, they were not guilty of fraud in altering their transcripts, they did not even break the rules of eligibility. No, they were guilty only of overemphasis. It was, after all, a benign term, an indiscretion rather than a misdemeanor. Their only sin was that they cared too much.

The term "overemphasis" became part of a developing lexicon, in much the same fashion that "overreaction" and "overzealousness" would be used a generation later to explain, if not justify, the wanton use of power and force. It was as if the most difficult of concepts could be properly distilled simply by manipulating the language. Quantification was America's manner of responding to all questions that could not be immediately answered. Quantum physics could serve as a substitute for metaphysics; behavioral analysis could circumvent the mysteries of the unconscious; and operationalism could certainly explain what was beyond the reach of ontology. It was easier that way, for if a problem could be quantified, the solution was at hand. If the massacre of hundreds of Vietnamese peasants was the result of over-zealousness, one could adjust by being somewhat less zealous. If American citizens were brutalized on the streets of Chicago because the police overreacted, then all that was needed was to temper the reaction. And if overemphasis of athletics was the reason why college kids took bribes, one could compensate by simply tightening the spigots.

The concept of overemphasis served mainly to salve the lesions of guilt. The truth was that games were being dumped not only in Madison Square Garden, but in midwestern field houses, and local gyms, and neighborhood schoolyards. And no degree of de-emphasis would change that. Following the scandal, every conceivable step was taken to de-emphasize the sport. New regulations were put into effect, codes were tightened and strictly enforced, tougher laws were passed. Within a month of the scandal's breaking, the Wicks-Mailler bill was passed into law, doubling the penalty for bribing a participant in an athletic contest to ten years in jail. The Senate passed a bill by Harold I. Panken, a Manhattan Democrat, making it a misdemeanor to induce anyone under the age of twenty-one to gamble. Assemblyman William W. Rosenthal introduced a bill in the California State Assembly that would make point shaving a felony offense. None of it helped. Ten years later, a nationwide point-shaving scandal broke that was of broader dimensions and wider scope. It involved more gamblers, more players, and more institutions than its predecessor, and though it spanned the nation, its nerve center was New York

City, and its putative head was no less a figure than Jack Molinas, Columbia's highscoring sophomore of 1951, who had seen it all happen the first time. The events of the fifties—the heartbreak, the broken careers, the jail terms—would prove to be no lessons at all. The new laws, the stiffer penalties, the de-emphasis of college athletics did not provide the effect of deterrence. The root of the scandal of the fifties conceivably ran through some unexplored terrain.

The seventeen players arrested between February and April did not constitute a very heterogeneous group. They were all in their late teens or early twenties. With two exceptions, they had grown up in the boroughs of New York—most of them in Brooklyn or the Bronx —attending city high schools and learning to play basketball in neighborhood schoolyards and playgrounds. They were mainly children of the prewar middle class, the sons of immigrants and first-generation Americans whose ancient roots were known only by inference: tailors and bakers and shoemakers, artisans of every description whose dreams were as modest as their means. They would work hard through the days of their lives, counting their change with care, and buoyed by a vision as profound as it was fundamental. Their sons would have a better life. They would receive an education; they would go to college and study hard and possibly become doctors or lawyers or teachers or deans. "My son is a professional man," they would be able to say. They saw themselves perhaps as second-leg runners in a relay race. They could not win the race themselves, but if they ran hard and tirelessly, the next leg would have an easier run once the baton was passed. The deprivations of one generation would be the nutrient of the next. So they worked and they watched. They observed with care, they advised, they instructed, passing on the lessons they had learned at their own deep but narrow fountains of wisdom. You must apply yourself, they would tell their sons, you have to study, work hard, make something of yourself. It was all the legacy they could hope to leave. Their children would carry their Old World values into the towers of some higher calling.

So their sons—the teen-age street kids of postwar America—were heir to a set of values that had been smuggled across half a continent and a breadth of ocean. The values, of course, were sound and simple and as safe as home cooking, but they left little to the imagination. They suggested a life without risk or gamble or the first element of danger. One's heroes did not live that way. Hemingway did not write about such characters, and John Garfield did not play them in the movies. The heroes of the streets did not bend to authority, they braced against it, they challenged it, they dared, there was a chancy swagger to their mood. If life was tough, one would have to be tougher; the world must be forced to make room. No, one could not quickly adopt a set of imported values whose first caveat was to hedge all bets and play it safe.

Of course, he could not easily give it up either, for it is the fundament of middle-class morality that it is never unreasonable; it never exceeds the restraints of logic. It does not invoke the curses of demons and spooks, it does not ordain sainthood or offer the promise of miracles. Its precepts are basic and its aims are practical. One might, if he chose, flee the cell of Southern Baptist dogma with the suddenness of a jailbreak, for its doctrines must be either accepted or renounced. But middle-class morality will not let go, it clings. One is obliged to work his way through it as if trapped in a sea of molasses. So one might wish to defy it without ever really relinquishing it, to stretch its boundaries just so far, so that its rewards might yet be forthcoming but on terms that did not bind. It would be possible, then, to maintain a dual citizenship; to hold hands with the devil while still waving the flag of the Lord.

The mute underworld of the streets held no small allure for these middle-class renegades. It was, after all, a world ideally suited to one's needs. One would not be sucked into the swirl of hit men or muggers or dope pushers. It was the world of polite crime—bookmakers, gamblers, nothing more than an occasional short term for assault. It was precisely the climate one needed, for it was possible to glide through it and still step out. One could spend the afternoon in the schoolyard or poolroom in company with neighborhood folk heroes who had seen the inside of a station house, he could get down a small bet at Bickford's and be privy to talk of point spreads and fixes, he could walk the narrow ledge that circled the abyss and still know that his roots were anchored in ground safe and hallowed. At home, one could live up to all expectations, but once outside, in the streets, he could leave behind the identity he wanted most to shed: he would not be the nice Jewish boy from the Bronx.

So the values of the middle class warred with the values of the streets, and the fictional heroes of the postwar decade were those who had won or lost the same battle, such as James Cagney in *White Heat,* a convict as hard and as tough as worn leather who cried openly when he learned that his mother had died; and John Garfield, one of our own from the streets of the Bronx, who dealt with gamblers and hoods but could not finally be bought. One would puzzle some years later at the popularity of their successors in the early sixties—an array of anti-heroes and government men like James Bond, who was a serial number and the product of technology. He had no roots, James Bond, he came from nowhere, he stood for nothing, he was the agent of authority. We required some dimension, some complexity, of our heroes, a connection to some firmer reality. There was, it would seem, the seminal knowledge that true values were always ambiguous. They could not be inherited, but would have to be earned, appropriated a piece at a time. The morality of the middle class, bright coin of lost generations and fugitive exiles, could not be possessed without first being renounced.

Still, the notion of dumping a basketball game could not have come easily to kids who had learned the game in New York's school-yards. Flirtations with the underworld, fleeting associations with gamblers and bookmakers, did not abuse the image one had of oneself. Basketball was a city game, and the kids who played it were of the cities, a part of the cast-iron world of knights and knaves, urban minstrels who could transform the staccato beat of a ball against concrete into an adagio suited to the ear of a royal court. But dumping a game did violence to every instinct that drove the wheels of one's self-respect. For the game of basketball, more than any other team sport, set one man against another in a confrontation as fierce as any outside the prize ring. One's reputation was the collateral in every encounter and each basket was the equivalent of a spike driven into the armor of one's opponent. One gave nothing away in a schoolyard game, and he could hope for nothing in return.

Of course, asking a player to control the score of a game, to stay within the spread, was not quite the same as asking him to lose it. It is not likely that many of the players could have been bribed to dump games outright. But a quality player could hold something back and still outscore his opponent, even be the game's high scorer. The point spread, in effect, added a whole new dimension to the game. It afforded the possibility of winning twice—of winning both the game and the bet—and only a player thoroughly secure in the refinements of his skill could hope to answer the challenge. For each time a player agreed to fix a game, he knew he would be required to transcend his athlete's gifts and distill them into those of the virtuoso. It would not be enough just to win, to dominate and finally conquer one's opponent. The aesthetic of style was now a factor. One would be obliged to pick the manner and moment of the kill in much the same way that the best of matadors will enter the terrain of the bull and dare the horns before administering the final stroke. The ingredient of magic lives in such a moment. If, in the purity of its form, basketball already bore some resemblance to improvised ballet, then the best of its performers might conceivably nurse the unconscious ambition to set roots in the land of the artist.

A decade later, a promising young heavyweight would take some pride in announcing before a fight the precise round in which he would stop his opponent. Perhaps it was no accident that each forecast was delivered in verse, for he was, he might have known, invoking the craft of the poet. There could be not the smallest margin for error. If the eighth round was chosen, he might have to carry the other fighter for two or three rounds, allowing his opponent no undue privileges and trying to win each round convincingly while taking care that it would not be the last, all the time waiting for the appointed moment, the precise three-minute segment in which he said he would finish the fight. It was not altogether different from shaving the points of a basketball game. He was making the fight closer than it might have been and, in the process, risking the prospect of sudden defeat. It was a delicate procedure, as brittle as the intent to win a basketball game by fewer than four points. But in the process he would learn, finally, something of what it was like to walk the long high wire that stretched the distance between soap opera and art. In the soul of every athlete resides the mood of the mystic.

The point spread, in fact, was not lacking in versatility. It could serve the needs of those who would abolish gambling as effectively as those who lived by it. For in the aftermath of the scandal, the "diabolical point spread," as it was sometimes called, was the subject of much conjecture. It was as if there were no gamblers, no bookmakers, no fixers, no players in need of some easy money. The point spread was treated as the cause of the scandal, and its elimination was seen not only as necessary but as sufficient to put an end to gambling and thus salvage the sport.

"If the point spread doesn't go," said Bobby Sand, the Phi Beta Kappa assistant coach of City College, "the game will. It's as simple as that."

It was not quite so simple. The point spread has endured and so has the game, largely unchanged, for a quarter century. The betting on college basketball is greater now than it ever was, and the line on each game is still readily accessible. If point shaving has become less prevalent, or disappeared entirely, it is only because the prospect of generous professional contracts places too high a price tag on a player's services. It is no longer worth the risk. But every contest is still played as a game within a game. The point spread remains intact. Big-time college basketball could not survive without it.

PART
FOUR

The dream died gently and without protest. On May 1, the Board of Higher Education issued a report barring City and all other municipal colleges from playing in Madison Square Garden or any other commercial arena. It also prohibited the recruitment of athletes and any preferential treatment to varsity players at City, Brooklyn, Queens, and Hunter colleges, and limited the number of hours that could be devoted to play and practice. Henceforward, the statement said, team members will be "students who play and not players who register." At the same time that it denounced commercialism and overemphasis, the Board also invoked what it called the doctrine of individual responsibility. It was a doctrine that was basic in its substance but ambitious in its claims. As each individual asserts the responsibility for his own acts, the Board said, "he can in one moment of speaking and action defeat evil." The doctrine, like the statement itself, served mostly to remind one that it was easier to identify the problem than it was to solve it.

The ban on recruitment was, of course, nothing more than a reaffirmation of an existing policy that some schools had chosen to ignore. The Board did not offer any new guidelines for enforcement or prescribe penalties in the event of violation or even indicate the number of hours of play and practice that would be considered to be within proper limits. The report, then, was a random mixture of the prosaic and the sublime whose only operational thrust was to place Madison Square Garden off limits to municipal colleges.

That was the end of it then. You knew now that you would never play basketball in the Garden. Never. The sweet revery that so often had brought solace on sleepless nights would be from then on an indulgence you could no longer afford. For with the last sliver of hope gone, the dream would assume, always, the cast of either self-pity or glorification. Visions that had no root in reality became bronzed instead in the imagination, embellished by new touches that you would not previously have dared.

Since the hope had always been a fragile one, the scenario had remained modest. You would see yourself on the bench for most of the game, looking up at the crowd in the steep decks above the medieval battlements, watching the hands on the multiple Garden clocks—one clockface for minutes, another for seconds, you had never learned to read them properly—but you would be watching them now and hoping there was still time left. Then the coach would motion toward you and call out the name of the man you were to replace, and you would shed your sweat suit and go to the scorer's table to report the substitution, and then remain there at midcourt, kneeling on one knee, waiting for a time-out or a foul to be called. And then the moment would come. You would hear the hoarse sound of the buzzer, and then your name would be announced to a crowd at Madison Square Garden, to all of New York, and you would shuffle out onto the shiny hardwood, onto the bright warm face of that hallowed court; a votary finally welcomed by the keepers of the faith.

That is the way you had always seen it. Sometimes a flourish or two would be added, a flurry of two or three clean shots near game's end or a behind-the-back pass that drew applause from the crowd. But now, now that the hope was gone the restraints were lifted. The scenario was due for revision. The role of last-minute substitute need no longer suffice. Now your introduction to the Garden would come at the start of the NIT. A spotlight was used to introduce the players before each game in a national tournament, and now you could see yourself in that light dribbling slowly out to midcourt. The pale lavender hue that washes down from the balcony is draped across your back like a royal mantle. The faint pool of tinted light is a halo at your feet that tracks your steps to the center circle. There, you stop, turn, and roll the ball back slowly to the bench.

So the opening round of the NIT was the new setting, and once the initial leap was made who could tell what summits might yet be scaled? It was not beyond hope to think you could be high scorer in any game you started, for when your finger warmed to the trigger you could shoot the nets off the basket; you knew that. Hadn't you once scored thirty-eight points in a game? It was only a night-center game, but still, you had made fourteen of fifteen shots from the floor and ten straight from the foul line. What difference did it make where the game was played? The baskets in the Garden were no higher than those in the Creston gym. They were ten feet high and eighteen inches in diameter no matter where the game was played.

But that was the breeziest of reveries; it had no substance, no definition. Your taste was for something with a bit more context. There were many scripts that suited, but your favorite found you at the foul line after time had run out. You had two shots and your team trailed by a point, and you could win the game or lose it now, alone on the Garden floor, naked and solitary before eighteen thousand of your own. It would be, you thought, like confronting eternity, for it was no longer a test of man against man; it was just you and the ball and the basket, a measure not of skill but of nerve, and you had always suspected, even then you had suspected that it was just such moments that offered a purchase on a slice of salvation. So you would stand out there alone, looking up into the balcony from where you so often had looked down, spinning the ball lightly in your hands, feeling for that one part of the surface that was grooved to your touch, and then, with a smooth, sudden rhythm, you would flick it cleanly through the hoop —once, twice—like wind whispering across the strings of a lyre. Swish, it would say, swish.

Yes, it was easy to conjure such pictures now, to savor the taste of lost glories, for you could no longer be held accountable. You did not, after all, try and fail; the opportunity had been stolen from you, smuggled and locked away before you ever had the chance to stake your slim claim. Small wonder, then, that the bitterness of disappointment was banked against the relief one felt at having been spared the possibility of failure.

The timing of the Board's statement was near to perfect. Just hours before its release, twelve former players from City, LIU, and NYU were indicted by the grand jury on charges of bribery and conspiracy for accepting $26,500 in payoffs from Salvatore Sollazzo. The players —Gard, Roth, Roman, Warner, Layne, Smith, Bigos, White, Feurtado, Miller, Lipman, and Schaff—all pleaded not guilty before Judge Saul S. Streit in the Court of General Sessions. Three other players —Mager, Dambrot, and Cohen—had not yet been indicted, Hogan said, because he lacked sufficient corroborating evidence. They had received their money not from Sollazzo but from Eli Kaye, who was still in Florida fighting extradition. But it was only a matter of time now.

On May 4, Kaye waived extradition, and his arrival in New York brought the first major turn in the case. For immediately after his indictment, bail was reduced from seventy-five to fifty thousand dollars, and he was permitted to return to Florida. None of the other fixers—not Sollazzo or Gard or Goldsmith—had been granted such liberties. They had not been permitted to leave the jursdiction of the court. Clearly, Kaye was the first who had demonstrated a willingness to cooperate. And while he was in Florida, Mager, Dambrot, Cohen, Roman, and Roth became the first to plead guilty to charges of fixing basketball games. It was a move that was not without wider implications, for it suggested that the case was being adjudicated outside the courts. Exchanges had been made; something had been conceded and something gotten in return.

For the judicial machine is tuned to run on more than one gear. Its switches are set to the wheels of compromise, and the first requirement of a good district attorney is that he be able to negotiate. There are very few cases that are decided entirely in the trial courts. Most are worked out, in their essentials, at bargaining sessions between prosecutors and defense attorneys. It begins at the time of arraignment, where bail is set according to the "reliability" of the defendant, and it proceeds through a period of plea bargaining. Since even the pettiest crimes are susceptible to more than one charge, the district attorney begins each session with a handful of the very best playing cards. The object, always, is to dispense justice while sparing the courts the inconvenience of a trial. It is not unlike a session of three-handed pinochle, in which the majority of games are won or conceded before the hand is actually played.

So the deal was worked out and consummated finally in the Court of General Sessions on July 5. Fourteen of the players—all except Eddie Gard—changed their pleas to guilty on a charge of conspiracy, and in return the court dismissed the bribery indictment. It was a fair enough exchange. The conspiracy charge was a misdemeanor, and carried with it an indeterminate prison term with a maximum of three years. Bribery was a felony. Conviction brought a minimum of two years in prison and possibly as many as ten. Perhaps more important, it meant that those convicted would bear the stigma of felons and would forfeit some of the privileges of citizenship. The distinction was not insignificant.

"We do not believe the public interest requires that these young men receive felony convictions," Assistant DA O'Connor explained. "In our view justice is adequately served by the acceptance of misdemeanor pleas from them."

Of course, the sentence that attended the misdemeanor convictions—commonly referred to as "pen indef"—gave added leverage to the courts. A defendant knew that the length of the sentence he received would likely bear direct relation to what he could offer the court in return. The judicial system functions on the grease of collateral and exchange, and the players had capital in abundance. Sollazzo was the district attorney's principal quarry, and the case against him rested heavily on testimony that only the players could provide. They agreed to turn state's evidence. Gard, who did not appear in court with the other players, was scheduled to go on trial with Sollazzo. But

O'Connor noted that he expected to dispose of Gard's case, in similar fashion, within the next few days.

The charge to which the players pleaded guilty was in itself a questionable one, for the conspiracy laws did not have roots in the highest ground of legal precedent. Most of them were, in fact, of recent vintage, the product of a time when some importance was attached to the possibility of apprehending suspects before they actually had committed a crime. The players, in effect, had confessed to conspiring, to planning, to fix basketball games, but not finally to fixing them. It meant that they could have been convicted even if the deal had never been closed and no game had ever been fixed. So the conspiracy laws opened a back door to the halls of justice, but few complaints would be heard from the players. They found that the legal structure was indeed a pliable instrument; it served those who knew best how to use it.

Sollazzo, of course, was not granted the same plea-bargaining privileges as the players, but a week later, after a special panel of jurors had already been chosen, he too changed his plea. Appearing in court with Gard, Sollazzo pleaded guilty to twenty-seven counts of bribery and one of conspiracy. He pleaded not guilty to two other bribery charges, and they were dismissed. But that probably was not the only concession made to Sollazzo. The bribery convictions each carried maximum terms of ten years in jail and fines of ten thousand dollars. So Sollazzo faced the possibility of spending the rest of his life behind bars, and it is not likely he would have consented to plead guilty unless he was given some assurance that his sentence would be considerably lighter. Gard, who had spent ten weeks in jail before being released, also announced his intention to plead guilty and testify for the state.

All that remained of the case, then, was the sentencing, which was scheduled for the fall. In the meantime, the NCAA, always quick to the heart of a problem, announced that its tournament would be withdrawn from Madison Square Garden. The eastern regionals would be played instead in the great eastern cities of Chicago and Raleigh, North Carolina. A number of big-time colleges—Bradley included—already had announced their intention to shun the Garden because of its "unsavory atmosphere." It was important, after all, to keep the games out of the East, which was known to be a melting pot of gamblers, bookmakers, and corrupt basketball players. Also, Chicago was just a shout and a whistle from Peoria, home of Bradley and the very model of small-town rectitude. Bradley, however, would not be the first to profit from the switch. For on July 24, just weeks after the announcement was made, it was disclosed that virtually the entire Bradley team of the grand-slam season—with the notable exceptions of Paul Unruh and Elmer Behnke—had fixed at least three basketball games, two of which were played in its Peoria field house.

Seven Bradley players—Gene Melchiorre, Bill Mann, Bud Grover, Aaron Preece, Jim Kelly, Fred Schlictman, and Mike Chianakas—were implicated in a point-shaving scandal that spanned the 1948–49 and 1949–50 seasons. In each of the two games played in Peoria, Bradley was able to win and still stay under the spread. The first was a 69–67 victory over Washington State on December 21, 1949. The second fixed contest was played almost a year later, on December 7, 1950, with Bradley winning a 77–74 decision over Oregon State.

The day after the Oregon State game, the headline in the *Peoria Star* read: "Bradley Turns Back Oregon State Revival 77–74; Squeak, Fred Count 21 Apiece." Squeak was Gene (Squeakie) Melchiorre, and Fred was Fred Schlictman. So two of the players who were shaving points were good enough to share high-scoring honors while both winning the game and beating the spread.

But things went less smoothly for Bradley in the one game they tried to fix in Madison Square Garden. It was the third-place consolation game of the 1949 National Invitation Tournament, and the Braves had agreed to dump the game outright, to lose to favored Bowling Green by seven or more points. Bradley was trailing by precisely seven when a substitute hit a long push shot at the buzzer to cut Bowling Green's margin to 82–77. The shot cost three Bradley players—Melchiorre, Mann, and Chianakas—five hundred dollars apiece, but the price they paid for the Bowling Green game would be even higher, for no other reason than that the game was played in New York. For although Illinois's bribery laws were tougher than New York's, the Peoria courts were not. In New York, the players would be obliged to go the full legal route, while in Peoria they were not even required to post bond. They were released in their own recognizance, and Melchiorre, who was the contact man, was treated not much differently from the others.

Melchiorre had orchestrated the Bradley operation right from the start. He met with gamblers in both Chicago and New York, he arranged the deals, settled on the price, collected and distributed the payoff money. His first dealings were with agents for Eli Kaye, but the gambling hierarchy was less tidy in the Midwest than it was in New York. The competition among rival gamblers was dogged and without restraint. It went beyond the niceties of competitive bidding. There were kidnappings, death threats, double crosses, transfers of bets; switches were made when the players were already on the court. The midwestern enterprise was a jagged network whose lines crossed and parted from nerve centers as far apart as New York and Kansas City. Each time the investigation was thought to have reached the top, it was discovered that the chain led elsewhere, even higher. This was not the orderly world of eastern corruption, of white-collar crimes like tax fraud and forgery. Involved here were gunmen and bank robbers, narcotics dealers and murder suspects, hard-edged thugs whose criminal lineage ran to the likes of Marty Krompier and Dutch Schultz.

Melchiorre, of course, had no direct dealings with them. His principal contacts were two brothers—Nicholas and Anthony Englisis—both from Brooklyn. The brothers worked as intermediaries first for Kaye and then for another ring, headed by Jack (Zip) West. But their allegiance crossed over, they got caught in a switch, and Anthony almost paid with his life.

Bradley had come East for a series of games in January 1950, and Kaye tried to arrange a fix against Manhattan in Madison Square Garden. But the players declined the offer because they felt that a convincing win would clinch a bid to the NIT. Bradley rolled over

Manhattan by twenty-two points, and the players were ready to do business on the next game, against St. Joseph's. Kaye and Nicholas Englisis followed the team to Philadelphia, and it was agreed that Bradley would stay under the spread. But West learned that the game had been fixed, and within hours major bookmakers were flooded with money on St. Joseph's. The point spread dropped sharply just before game time, and Kaye figured he had been double-crossed. He decided to switch his bet to Bradley. Melchiorre was instructed to try to win the game and cover the points. Again word got back to West, but it was too late for him to switch his bets. He was already down heavily on St. Joseph's, and now he faced the possibility of losing it all on a fix that was going the other way.

But West had a degree of imagination when it came to fixing a game, and he had the means to carry it through. He arranged for two musclemen to bring Anthony Englisis to his apartment on Bay Parkway in Brooklyn, and informed him that he would not leave the apartment alive if Bradley covered the spread. Anthony phoned Convention Hall in Philadelphia and had his brother paged from among the fifteen thousand spectators. He told him to change the deal again. The players were already warming up. Nicholas caught Melchiorre's eye and signaled thumbs down. Melchiorre nodded. Anthony was kept locked in the bathroom of the second-floor apartment until West learned that Bradley had won the game 64–60, two points under the spot. Then he was given a drink, one thousand dollars in cash, and released. Kaye took a big loss on the game, and he realized, of course, that he had been sold out. A year and a half later he evened the score. He told the story to the district attorney's office in New York.

Bradley fixed only one more game that season, and it almost cost the team its place in the NCAA tournament and the chance for a rematch with City. The game was the one against Kansas for the District Five NCAA berth, and Bradley very nearly lost it. They trailed in the closing minutes until Paul Unruh scored three field goals in forty-five seconds to give Bradley a 59–57 decision. They had entered the game a four-point favorite, won by two, and netted their sponsors an estimated eighty thousand dollars in betting capital. It apparently was too close a call for Melchiorre. He decided he wanted out, and reportedly turned down a ten-thousand-dollar package to lose to City in the NCAA finals.

The ten-thousand-dollar offer came close to equaling the total amount paid to seven Bradley players over a two-year period. They had, for the most part, been fixing games for five hundred dollars apiece. The same figure was the standard rate of payment for four players on the University of Toledo team, who disclosed that they had fixed four games during the 1950–51 season. The Toledo script did not differ very much from Bradley's. The players were working for the same gamblers, they too had crossed Kaye in favor of West, and there were similar tales of near misses, double-dealing, and veiled threats.

So the going rate in the Midwest was apparently only half of what it took to fix a player for one of the New York colleges. But if that was the first distinction to be noted, it was not the most telling. The reaction to the scandals was quite different in each section of the country, and so were the actions taken by the school administrations, the grand juries, and the courts. The sense of outrage, the mood of recrimination, had been profound in the Midwest when it was believed that only New York City schools had been involved.

"Out here in the Midwest, this condition, of course, doesn't prevail," Phog Allen had said, "but in the East, the boys . . . are thrown into an environment which cannot help but breed the evil which more and more is coming to light."

Allen, of course, had no way of knowing then to what extent this condition did prevail in the Midwest. He did not know that a year earlier his Kansas team had been able to stay close to Bradley because Bradley was dumping, not in New York, not in Madison Square Garden, but in the sanctuary of a midwestern field house. Allen's statement was made on the very same day that Bradley voted unanimously to reject a bid to the NIT in order to avoid the "unsavory atmosphere" of the Garden.

So a New Yorker, whose faith had been trampled and whose own wish to play in the Garden was crushed before the first shot was taken, might have asked pardon if he felt some small sense of vindication on learning that the hallowed precincts of the Midwest, sacramental seat of high American virtue, were as corrupt as the bleakest alley of a Brooklyn tenement. He might also express a degree of surprise when no new sermons were forthcoming and when coaches and administrators who had spoken earlier with the righteous assurance of country preachers now found it fitting to temper their judgments with forgiveness.

Adolph Rupp, of Kentucky, who had proclaimed that gamblers "couldn't reach my boys with a ten-foot pole," came suddenly to the realization that fixing the scores of basketball games was really not so serious after all. "The Chicago Black Sox threw games," Rupp said, "but these kids only shaved points."

The administration at Bradley issued its first major statement on the scandal one week after its players confessed. The announcement was to the effect that Bradley would continue to pursue its complete athletic program "with the natural hope that our teams will win." The statement was promulgated with the inspiration of the Bradley Booster Club and with the blessing of the university's president, David Blair Owen. Of course, precautions would be taken. Officials of the university would keep closer supervision, they would screen visitors to the dormitories, they would keep their players from going to New York City. In effect, the Bradley administration took no action at all. City College had canceled the remainder of its basketball schedule. LIU had abandoned its athletic program entirely. All of the New York schools that were implicated took steps to deemphasize sports, to curtail the recruitment of athletes, to limit subsidization. The measures might have been ineffective, even somewhat naïve, but they were at least the expression of deep hurt and disillusion, an acknowledgment of a degree of responsibility and a faint call to conscience. Bradley did nothing at all. What was a crime in New York was little more than an indiscretion in Peoria.

But then the life of New York, its very existence, did not ever seem to depend on the success or failure of its college teams. The sport of basketball was taken seriously and more than a little pride was invested in its own, but there were other ways by which a New Yorker could measure his identity. Small towns survive on blood that is siphoned from their college and high school teams. It is the only wire that attaches them to a world that is larger than Main Street. Who would ever have heard of Peoria if it were not for Bradley University? And who would have heard of Bradley were it not for its basketball team? To the rest of the country, Peoria was not a city, it was a basketball site, the Home of the Braves, and without them who would know the difference between Peoria and Paducah? So while the texture of intercollegiate sports was altered forever in New York, it remained unchanged at Bradley, and the players would find the distinctions between the two legal systems to be no less profound.

Immediately after their arrest, the Bradley players had been warned to come to New York to testify or face indictment in absentia and eventual extradition by the Illinois governor, Adlai E. Stevenson. The five players wanted—Melchiorre, Mann, Chianakas, Grover, and Preece—consented, and they were questioned for three hours on August 15. Two days later, Melchiorre, Mann, and Chianakas were indicted for their part in fixing the game with Bowling Green at Madison Square Garden. Grover and Preece were not involved in that game, and they were cleared. The three named in the indictment all eventually pleaded guilty and received suspended sentences of indeterminate terms up to three years. In Peoria, where two of the fixed games had been played, where all the deals were consummated, where the penalties were harsher, and where even failure to report a bribe attempt was a criminal offense, the grand jury indicted only Melchiorre, on charges arising out of the Oregon State game. Preece, Kelly, and Schlictman, who were implicated in the same game, were acquitted on grounds they had already suffered enough mental, physical, and financial hardship. The charges in the Washington State game were dismissed entirely. Even Melchiorre's indictment and conviction resulted only in his being placed on probation for a year. And quick as that, the show closed in Peoria.

Yet Melchiorre had been more than just another point shaver. He was the contact man for two groups of gamblers, he had arranged the fixes, set up the players, collected and distributed the money. In New York, players who filled lesser roles served jail terms, and the colleges were as unbending as the courts. Four days after the Peoria grand jury failed to indict three of the four Bradley players, City College denied reinstatement to Roman, Warner, Roth, Layne, and Cohen, pending final disposition of their cases. But Peoria was quick to wipe the slate clean, and Bradley continued its basketball program as if nothing had happened.

Small Town, USA, could be trusted always to look after its own, for a crime committed by one of its sons, no matter how great or how small, was felt as a curse breathed upon the town itself. It was the first injunction of small-town psychology that the enemy always lay somewhere outside its own gates. And so if kids from Peoria, Illinois, had accepted bribes from gamblers to fix basketball games, they had not learned to do it in Small Town. Such corruption, such moral taint, did not breed in the wide-open spaces of America's heartland. It festered in the midnight shadows, in the cracks and crevices of big-city streets.

For decades, small-town America had lived in quiet terror of the big city. It was not just the change in rhythm, the accelerated tempo of big-city beats that spoke of menace in the air, nor even the cool sense of displacement that comes from living and moving among strangers. It was something deeper than that, a force more primitive than fear that fell and hardened like ice across the heart of small-town transients. For in the big city life always walked the edge of the unknown. Around each new corner lay a snakepit of possibilities for which nothing in one's past might have offered preparation. And so life in the big city obliged one to be ready to discover something new about himself with the coming of each day. His identity was never complete, it could never be wholly known, for the life he lived was without final definition. If he wished to think of himself as being brave, he knew that tomorrow he might be asked to test his courage with the glint of cold steel beating at his eye. If he thought of himself as a man of deep feeling, he would soon discover whether he was the one to pause and stoop or whether he too would step over the fallen figure at the base of the subway stairs. The big city did not leave many questions open. It was a vise that tightened down upon the nerves until one was forced to respond, until he would grudgingly confess that perhaps he was not as good or as brave as he had hoped. No, life in the big city offered no promise of rest. It stalked one through the canyons of the most shapeless dread, and if one had an eye for the summit, he knew that he must first offer greetings to the demons of the deeps.

And small-town America was not ready to close such a pact. It thrived on an identity that was immune to the passing of time, for in every small town there was the umbilical knowledge that where time could be deprived of change, life could be lived without peril. The small town, after all, had as its ancestor the walled village of the primitive past, where the most lethal powers were invested in forces that could not be known. Small Town understood.

So if the Welcome Wagon greeted each new neighbor with a smile and a how-do, it was not only the ease and comfort of the new arrival that were served. One could trust that a degree of intelligence about the new family on the block might yet be carried back into the neighborhood. One was eager to know them, of course, for one did not wish to live among strangers. Yes, it was not unlikely that the root of small-town friendliness, the neighborly face that it turned toward the door, was imbedded in the hard rock of the darkest suspicions. Xenophobia lived at the doorstep of every house on Main Street, and not without cause. For in its dogged desire for self-preservation, Small Town had backed itself to the very edge of paranoia. It could protest its innocence in the daylight, if it chose, but its nights would be alive with spooks. If we will not acknowledge our own sins, the voice whispered, there will always be others ready to accuse us. But then how many were prepared to heed the musings of a voice in the dark? No, the judgments of Small Town would be cast by none but its own.

And so Peoria could not only forgive, but also pardon, the sons who had trespassed against it. New York of course could not, because it had seen itself for half a century not so much as a city but as the geocentric pivot of a nation's conscience, and such conscience was obliged always to live by its own rules. New York had never belonged to itself as Peoria did. It did not subsist on the turn of its own generations. It was the common property of those who chanced to come, a city of the world, and its deeds were seen as parables that gave some suggestion of how things ought to be. And so New York would be the first to pay the price. It would send its own players to jail, it would take its own teams out of Madison Square Garden, it would suspend or de-emphasize its own athletic programs. But Small Town, America, took care of its own. It had raised its sons on good home cooking, and if they had gone to the big city and returned as thieves, well it was no fault of theirs, and Small Town would not punish them for Big City sins.

The gamblers involved in the case would not, of course, be among the beneficiaries of small-town largesse. The Peoria grand jury, while acquitting three of the four players, returned indictments against the Englisis brothers, Kaye, West, and four other fixers who were subsequently implicated. Still another suspect was held as a material witness, and his importance loomed large, for he was said to possess information on fixes as widespread as the Deep South and the Pacific Coast.

It was under a cloud of just such foreboding that workouts would soon begin for the 1951–52 season. Early in September, in an effort to clear the air, Attorney General J. Howard McGrath appointed a committee to conduct a nationwide investigation of the influence of sports gambling. The committee was headed by Francis T. Murray, director of athletics at the University of Pennsylvania. Other members, representing their various sports, were: Alfred Gwynne Vanderbilt, horse racing; Gene Tunney, boxing; Will Harridge and Ford Frick, baseball; Dana X. Bible, of the University of Texas, college football; Bert Bell, commissioner of the National Football League, professional football; Ned Irish, executive vice-president and director of basketball at Madison Square Garden, professional basketball; and Everett Dean, basketball coach at Stanford University, college basketball.

It was a distinguished committee, whose members no doubt knew a great deal about the sports they represented, but very little about gambling. Thus the investigation, which was said to be nationwide, was concluded within two weeks, and its findings were not unpredictable. The committee returned with five basic proposals: (1) stricter enforcement of anti-gambling laws; (2) uniform laws for all states; (3) abolition of betting pools; (4) an effort to heighten public awareness of the consequences of gambling; and (5) closer surveillance of players and their associates.

It was a report that did not seem to require so notable a committee or even two weeks of study, and it is not likely that it helped very much to restore public confidence. At the same time, the University of Kentucky's basketball team, NCAA champions of the previous season, was making a good-will tour that took it as far as Puerto Rico. The Kentucky team had turned over completely in the past two seasons, hardly missing a beat or a national title. The 1948–49 team had included Alex Groza, Ralph Beard, Dale Barnstable, Wallace (Wah-Wah) Jones, Jim Line, Cliff Barker, and Walter Hirsch. Now making the tour with their own NCAA championship were such as Frank Ramsey, Bobby Watson, Cliff Hagan, Shelby Linville, and of course the seven-foot All-American, Bill Spivey. Kentucky was as close as one could get to a perennial champion of college basketball. It had not been involved in so much as a whisper of scandal. One could not hope for a team better suited to the role of good-will ambassador.

It was a gambler's catechism in the late forties. The smart money knew never to bet against the Yankees in baseball, Notre Dame in football, or Joe Louis in boxing. A fourth entry might have been added to the list. During the first four postwar seasons, the University of Kentucky's basketball team played 140 basketball games and won 130 of them. It won a national tournament—either the NIT or NCAA—three times and was runner-up the fourth. The Wildcats of Kentucky were the finest of all college basketball teams, good enough for four of their starters and their number-one substitute to form their own professional team and earn a place in the NBA playoffs as rookies. But Kentucky was not always the choice of those inclined to wager on the outcome of the game. Though they had won 93 percent of their games over a four-year period, their percentage was not nearly so good against the spread. On October 20, 1951, the reason became apparent. Three of the starting five—Ralph Beard, Alex Groza, and Dale Barnstable—admitted that at least one of their ten defeats had come in a game they were paid to control, and it had been no ordinary contest. The game they had fixed was the opening round of the National Invitation Tournament on March 14, 1949.

It was the senior year for Beard and Groza and for two of the other starters—Wah-Wah Jones and Cliff Barker. Adolph Rupp had hoped —had even come close to predicting—that his team would be the first ever to win the NIT and the NCAA in the same season. It was not an idle wish. Kentucky had won twenty-nine of its thirty games during the regular season and its last twenty-one in a row. It was the defending NCAA champion, and with four of its five starters now in their senior year, the team was at the very peak of its performance. Kentucky had drawn a bye in the opening round and was installed a ten-point favorite over Loyola of Chicago in the quarterfinals, but it was beaten cleanly, 67–56. The Wildcats went on to win the NCAA tournament, but the chance for the double championship had already been lost. It had been sold for a total of fifteen hundred dollars, five hundred for each player.

It was not the only game with which the players had tampered. They had succeeded in shaving the points against the University of Tennessee in a game played in Kentucky's Alumni Gymnasium in Lexington, also for five hundred dollars a man, and they had received bonuses of one hundred dollars for running up the scores of three other games, all in their senior year. At least five other instances were cited in which the players had failed to deliver that season, and the games spanned the map of collegiate basketball—Chicago and New Orleans, Nashville and New York. Kentucky had been fixing games, successfully or not, in every part of the country they visited, in big-city arenas and small-town gyms and their own spanking-new four-million-dollar field house in Lexington. They had conspired with gamblers in more than one fourth of the games they played during the 1948–49 season.

It might have gone even deeper than that, but the degree of their involvement would never be known because the state of Kentucky had no law against the bribing of amateur athletes. And so the players were not obliged to answer a single question once they left the jurisdiction of New York. If half their games over a four-year period had been played at home, they were clear of the law on every one of them, whether they were dumping or not. They made only one trip a season to New York, except for tournament play, and they obviously were not about to make any admissions concerning games played in jurisdictions that were not conducting inquiries. So far as the record was concerned, then, Beard, Groza, and Barnstable received no more than thirteen hundred dollars in payoff money during their four-year careers, the last five hundred in exchange for losing an NIT game that deprived them of a chance for a tournament sweep in their final college season.

If that was the extent of it, one would have to believe that the most successful team in college basketball had either not been approached or had rebuffed the offers of bribes until their senior year. Then, with graduation just months away, with the promise of lucrative professional contracts in sight, they succumbed to the entreaties of gamblers, began abbreviated careers as point shavers at the rate of five hundred dollars a game, and failed to deliver in all but two attempts.

The chronicle was not a convincing one, not as a prelude to inviting defeat in the opening round of the NIT. Even assuming that the players felt they would have little difficulty defeating Loyola and still staying below a ten-point spread, it does not seem likely that they would have agreed to fix that game if they had succeeded only once before in beating the spread; not for five hundred dollars. A tournament sweep would have been worth many times that to a player about to turn pro. Gene Melchiorre had turned down a ten-thousand-dollar package rather than risk losing the NCAA final, and Melchiorre was, after all, a man with some experience. Yet here was Kentucky, acknowledged national champions, winners of gold medals in the 1948 Olympics, favorites to accomplish a feat at which no team had ever succeeded, ready to ransom its future for pocket money. If they were prepared for that kind of gamble, reason would dictate, it would have to be for a lot more than five hundred dollars; unless they had been fixing games on a regular basis for several seasons. For if they had, they might have become accustomed to the ease and exhilaration of winning twice, and conceivably they might have felt that they owed one more payday to those they had been doing business with over the past few years.

The losses incurred by Beard and Groza were substantial. Their professional basketball careers were snuffed out suddenly and completely; they were barred from the NBA for life. It was not easy to measure what it cost them. Just two years earlier, they had been part of an experiment that probably was unique in professional sports. Five graduating Kentucky players—Beard, Groza, Jones, Barker, and Joe Holland—had signed as a unit to form the newly organized Indianapolis franchise of the NBA. They signed for a fifty-thousand-dollar package and a share of the profits, for they would own and operate the team as well as play for it. Barker was the head coach, they were all officers of the corporation, and they owned 70 percent of the voting stock with an option to buy out the franchise within three years. The team had been an immediate success, both on the court and at the box office. They won their divisional championship as rookies and qualified for the playoffs in each of their first two seasons. And whether at home or on the road, they drew the crowds.

Their first game at Madison Square Garden was something of an occasion, more a homecoming than an appearance by a visiting team. If New York was devout in its partisanship to the home team, it was altogether secular in its appreciation of excellence. There had always been visiting players and teams that New York welcomed as its own, particularly when they had about them a Cinderella quality or an air of transcendence, and this team from Indianapolis had both. Just eight months earlier they had won the NCAA title on this same Garden floor, and now they were back as a team of freshmen in the toughest of all professional leagues.

The largest crowd ever to attend a pro game in the Garden— 18,135—turned out for the event, and you were among them, along with a legion of others from your neighborhood, your "block." You met in front of the corner candy store on Walton Avenue and 183rd Street, a familiar way station just four blocks from the Creston schoolyard, and there you waited for your numbers to swell, gathering in small clusters around the rickety newsstand with the weighted chain laid across the stacks of evening papers. And then, perhaps a dozen strong, you walked the three blocks to the Grand Concourse and took the Independent Subway to Fiftieth Street. There, in front of Nedick's, you met with still another group, from other blocks, and more than two hours before the game was to begin, you showed your G.O. card, paid seventy-five cents, and climbed to the balcony on the Eighth Avenue end of the Garden. You were not too early. More than an hour before game time every seat was filled, and the aisle in back of the very last row had begun to clog with standing-room-only.

It was the home opener for the Knicks, and you had come to root for Carl Braun and Harry Gallatin and for four new players—Dick McGuire, Vince Boryla, Ernie Vanderweghe, and Connie Simmons —who would turn the Knicks into a championship contender. But it was really the Kentuckians who drew you to the Garden that night, and the lustiest cheers of greeting were bestowed upon Ralph Beard and Alex Groza. Groza did more than earn them. He poured in forty-one points that night, almost half of what his team scored in an 83–79 victory. It was an astonishing performance for 1949, years before the twenty-four-second clock made one-hundred-point games commonplace. Groza played all forty-eight minutes, working in close to the basket against Connie Simmons, in what is known as a low post. The foul lanes had not been widened then, and they still resembled a keyhole, with the narrow lane leading to the foot of the circle, and Groza took his position as close to the basket as he could, usually on the right side of the lane, waiting for the ball to be fed to him by Ralph Beard or Wah-Wah Jones. When the ball came into the pivot, Groza would feint a pass to one of the breaking guards and then spin to his left for a hook shot that would be banked lightly off the glass. "Basket by Groza," the voice over the public-address system would say. Again and again it would come, with a monotony that generated excitement as you watched the totals mount. Simmons, who was about the same height as Groza's six feet seven, was perhaps twenty pounds lighter, and he was left helpless on those short tight turns to the basket. "Basket by Groza." You would hear the drone in your sleep that night and see, through the glass of the backboard, the number fifteen on the back of the jersey as it turned until you could glimpse the face and see the ball go up and then get sucked through the hoop in a naked caress. Basket by Groza.

Groza was named to the all-pro team that season, and he was joined on the team a year later by Ralph Beard. One more season and they would have been eligible to buy out the franchise. Groza might well have become the highest-paid player in professional basketball. Salaries were comparatively modest at the time. The highest-paid player in the NBA, George Mikan, was earning under twenty thousand dollars a year, and only a handful of the league's top stars were paid salaries in the range of five figures.

But the losses suffered by Beard and Groza could not be measured in terms of money. Basketball was the substance of life for both of them, and their banishment was the equivalent of an attorney being permanently disbarred after he had been graduated from law school, passed the bar, and completed the first two years of a successful practice. Really, it was even more severe, for a basketball player, like a concert pianist or a classical dancer, begins working at his craft when he is very young. Most start when they are just five or six years old, before their hands are large enough to hold a regulation-size ball or their limbs strong enough to reach a ten-foot-high basket. They work up to it slowly, clumsily straining for the hoop with underhand shots or hurling the ball shot-put fashion until they develop the strength and the grace to begin to refine their delicate skills—shooting from the outside, dribbling with either hand, driving to the basket —and then the even more tenuous intricacies of team play, beginning with moves that must be quick as fire and as subtle as the wind. They have invested fifteen years, almost all the years of their lives, in training and apprenticeship by the time they are ready to be paid for their labors.

Ralph Beard said he had started shooting baskets when he was a baby. "I'll tell you the truth," he told an interviewer in 1949. "My mother claims the first thing I used for a goal was my little old pottie. I wasn't a heck of a lot older, either, when I got my first real basket hung on the garage door. From then on, I was all set. We used to play some great games out there in the alley. We'd choose up sides as soon as we got out of school and go to it."

Beard trained and disciplined himself assiduously. His passion for physical fitness was so great and his training habits so rigorous that he drank nothing but water or tea. Even milk was verboten, he said, because milk can cut your wind. For as long as he could remember, Beard's life was built around basketball. "I just love it," he said, "I can't get enough of that game."

Beard played the game of basketball as though he were heir to private visions that had been the property of kings. At five feet ten, he performed in the backcourt like an impresario, moving the ball with a frantic suddenness, an invisible grace that suggested the complexity and the silent precision of a fine Swiss watch. Nimbly, he would feed the pivot or the corners and then break for the basket, seeking the three or four feet of unguarded space that offered the promise of passage. He would bank the lay-up with either hand, or shoot the two-hand set shot behind a screen, or mount his own rush to the hoop on a fast break, traveling the length of the court as if loose on some sacred mission. He was the patchwork embodiment of every skill a schoolyard player could wish to own.

Yet, off the court, he possessed few of the traits of the schoolyard sharp. He was a small-town boy, from Hardinsburg, Kentucky, and his manner was formal and polite, proud but still humble. He dressed well, he punctuated his sentences with "sir," and though he was sensitive about his height, he displayed little arrogance toward his critics. His size, small even by the standards of the forties, might have given Adolph Rupp a moment's pause when Beard entered his office for the first time. Rupp, who was known as the Baron of Basketball, was not nonchalant in his selection of players. Rumor had it that the doorway to his office was six feet two inches high, and that he gave little time to players who did not bump their heads on the way in. Rupp, in fact, had a reputation for recruiting and subsidizing athletes that had attracted criticism long before the first scandal broke. He had indeed built teams of awesome power. Within a five-year span, Kentucky won four national titles and three major tournaments, while undergoing a complete turnover in personnel. The team never seemed to be hurt by graduation or obliged to suffer the pangs of rebuilding.

Rupp, of course, denied the charge that he actively recruited and lavishly subsidized his players. They were "just a bunch of small-town boys," he said, "just some kids from down the road." But they all managed to find their way to the University of Kentucky. For the 1947–48 season, Kentucky built a four-million-dollar field house on its Lexington campus, with a capacity of twelve thousand, two thirds the size of Madison Square Garden and larger than most public arenas at the time.

Yet an article in the *Lexington Leader* observed that "basketball is purely a school sport around here. If they holler for more points during a game, it's just to break a new scoring record, not because they're worried about the point spread at the end." It was noted, too, that there was "very little betting" in a small community like Lexington and "absolutely no organized bookmaking such as you find in the larger population centers." The new field house was described as a civic asset that "will enable the Wildcats to take care of all the folks who want to see them play . . . and help the Athletic Association budget at the same time."

One well might wonder how an expenditure of four million dollars would help a university's budget or why a field house nearly the size of the Boston Garden was necessary in a town with a population of less than one hundred thousand. Yet the conviction endured that there was very little betting in small towns like Lexington, despite its proximity to Louisville, which was best known to the world for bourbon and racehorses. Was it really inconceivable to think that all those folks who sent hard cash through the pari-mutuel windows during the racing season might think to wager a dollar or two on the home team when Churchill Downs was closed? But no one felt the need to ask the question. The image of big cities is created by tourists and transients who make brief visits and return to Small Town with tales of horror and woe. But towns like Peoria and Lexington are not on the paths of many tour guides, and so their images are carried forth by the hometown folks. The likelihood is that there were more games fixed in the field houses of middle America than in the public arenas of all the big cities. It was just that in the cities it made a difference. Small towns write their own epitaphs.

The arrest of the Kentucky players no longer carried the capacity to shock. The fixing of college basketball games was regarded as an axiom of the sport by then, and if teams were shaving points in New York and Peoria, then why not in Kentucky? Besides, autumn was a month old by then, a new school year had started, a new season was approaching, and the scandals seemed to be a part of the past. You had more pressing concerns then, a set of priorities that included the possibility of beginning your own college basketball career. Tryouts were proceeding and the squad was being scaled down by the time the Kentucky players were arrested and flown East.

It was late October. The leaves were already off trees and they clung to the flagstone walks like freshly pasted mats. You can remember, so many years later, the rain and the dullness of the day and the wet leaves under your running feet. The gym building was in the southeast corner of the campus, and you went to it hurriedly and then up the stairs to the second floor where the list of names was pinned to the center of the bulletin board. There were fifteen names on it, and your own, in its proper alphabetical place, was fifth from the top. At the bottom was a note saying that the first practice session would be held at four o'clock that afternoon.

So you had gone that far at least, survived the last cut, won a place on a college team in the very last five minutes of tryouts. The coach finally had remembered your name. He had not known it the previous afternoon, the day of the final cuts, and the allotted time for scrimmage was running down.

"Has everyone been in?" the coach asked.

You stood up. He asked your name, and you told him.

"Go in for the redhead," he said.

You checked into the game, looked up at the clock, and you knew that the first time the ball touched your hands in the forecourt it would be on its way to the hoop. You had spent hundreds of hours playing basketball the past summer, much of it by yourself, shooting from every spot within range, until there was not a place on the court that was alien to your eye. You shot one-hand push shots until your arm was weary, until you grew tiny calluses on the tips of the fingers of your right hand. You worked alone, often in the darkness, because once you had picked your spot the vague shadow of the rim was target enough; the ball would find its way.

And now, in the space of five minutes, you would shoot three times at the bright orange rim, and each time, as the ball reached the peak of its arc and hung for a brief instant in airless space above the court, you would turn your back to the basket and start back down on defense, pausing at midcourt to watch the ball catch briefly in the netting before falling to the floor. After the third shot, there is the sound of the whistle ending the scrimmage.

"That's nice shooting," the coach says. "Do you always shoot that way?"

"Often enough," you tell him.

"What did you say your name was?"

"Cohen," you tell him.

Later, in the locker room, he stops by while you are dressing. "That really was nice shooting," he says again. Then he pauses. "Klein, right?"

You shake your head. "Cohen," you say. This time he writes it down.

So you would play basketball not for City but for Hunter College, which had only now opened its Bronx campus to men. It was a team composed entirely of freshmen, but it was the only team the school had, the first it had ever had, and the third-floor gym was filled to overflow for the opening game against Pace College. The game had been held up for about twenty minutes because the uniforms were late in arriving. They had been made to order, and they were delivered finally in large cartons; shiny purple-and-white uniforms with warm-up suits that had "Hunter" spelled out across the back in big block letters.

The team gathered outside the doors of the gym, and looking in through the small inset windows, you could see the stands and the balcony jammed tight with students, sitting in the aisles and standing in the rear, banners draped across the façade of the balcony, and when the double doors opened and the team came onto the floor in two files, the lead man dribbling for the basket at the far end of the court, the din was the equal of any you had ever heard. You could feel the vibrations come up through the floor and into your hands as you took your warm-up shots, but the tingling sensation you felt was not without pain, for the small finger of your left hand was broken in two places, and every step opened a core of pain that rode up into the arm and into the side of your head as hot and as fierce as the exposed nerve in a tooth. The finger had been fractured in a scrimmage and placed in a cast just two weeks earlier, but you had cut the cast away now because you did not want to miss playing in the team's first game. Still, it would not be an auspicious debut. You did not get into the game until midway through the second half, stayed just long enough to take a twenty-five-foot shot that went off the front rim, and left voluntarily with a misshapen finger that would have to be reset with the aid of diathermy. It was the start of a college basketball career that would be brief, often memorable, and entirely without distinction. But the season turned out to be a good one. The team finished with a winning record, and was good enough to beat the freshman teams of the other municipal colleges—City, Brooklyn, and Queens—in consecutive games. You were not, finally, unhappy about transferring from City.

The decision to switch had been made at the very last opportunity. You had already been admitted to City College, had in fact registered and paid the fee, and then, on an impulse as compelling as it was sudden, you bolted the campus, took the subway up to Bedford Park Boulevard, where, upon some hasty explanations, a degree of insistence, and the payment of a late fee, you were granted permission to transfer. You could not know why the impulse had struck the way it had, you would never know really, except that each visit to the City campus had brought with it an increasing sense of gloom and depression, as though one were visiting a home where someone had recently died. You did not wish to spend four years there. If college was, in its way, the beginning of a new life, one would sooner see it commence at a place which had no past.

City, with its very rich history, was preparing for its first "minor" basketball season in many years. Madison Square Garden was no longer part of its itinerary, most of the big-name colleges were gone from its schedule, and there was barely a recognizable name on its roster. If the prospects for the coming season held little promise at the start of the school year, they would grow even dimmer as the season drew near. Herb Holstrom, the co-captain and one of the few returning lettermen, was inducted into the Army early in November. That same day, three other City players were declared ineligible by the Eastern Collegiate Athletic Conference because they had played summer basketball in the Catskills. And on the day of the season opener against Roanoke, three more players, including co-captain Arnie Smith, were barred from competition on grounds that their records had been altered to grant them admission. The players denied any knowledge of tampering, and indeed, indications were that they had never seen their records. In any event, City, which had been stripped of four of its starters from the previous season, lost an additional seven players from its current team within three weeks of the opening of the 1951–52 season. The Beavers would not be much of a power, not even within the city, and Nat Holman was preparing to take a sabbatical at the end of the school year.

At around midseason, you saw Holman working a game from the City College bench. Your own Hunter team had played, and defeated, the City freshmen in a preliminary game, and you stayed around to watch the varsity. The winner of the game, even the opponent, are long since gone from memory, and all that remains is the picture of Holman, pink-faced and somber, his forehead wrinkled, hunched forward in his neat gray suit, motioning with a rolled-up program, moving players in and out of the game, and you could only wonder what he might be seeing then, what pale visions of past glories might be summoned from the vaults of memory and indulged for short periods of time, and at what cost. The brightest of his trophies, his grand-slam team, had already been irreparably tarnished. One of his players was in jail now, another was waiting to go, and five others had already been convicted and sentenced.

The sentencing was expected to be a routine procedure. Sollazzo, of course, would be obliged to serve time, and perhaps Gard, but no one expected any of the other players to receive jail terms. District Attorney Hogan had already solicited the clemency of the court. He suggested that sentence be suspended for all of the players, including Gard. The same request was made by Jacob Grumet, defense attorney for the City players, and by Nat Holman, Dr. Harry Wright, president, and Sam Winograd, faculty manager of athletics at City. Grumet pointed out that ninety West Point cadets, many of them members of Army's football team, had been expelled in a cribbing scandal a few months earlier, but were pardoned upon the urging of Cardinal Spellman. He said he hoped Judge Streit would be "guided by the same spirit."

In fact, one was hard-pressed to find a single case in which an athlete—amateur or professional—had been sent to jail for fixing a game. The Brooklyn College players of 1945 had been permitted to go free. Hank Poppe and Jack Byrnes, of Manhattan, received suspended sentences and were placed on probation. Even the Chicago Black Sox, who came near to sinking professional sports in America when they dumped the 1919 World Series, were spared jail terms, and that had not been a matter of college kids shaving points for pocket money. They were high priests of the national pastime, professional athletes throwing a World Series for as much as ten thousand dollars a man—more money than they earned a year—but the price they paid was professional rather than criminal. They were banished from baseball for life, their names were stricken forever from the record books, but they did not go to jail. And so precedent suggested nothing more than suspended sentences and a period on probation. But that was not the story waiting to be told.

It was late in the afternoon, just days before Thanksgiving and two weeks before the opening of the basketball season, and the week's first practice session had ended with a high-speed scrimmage. You had showered and dressed, and now, together with five or six others, you were in Joe's Luncheonette, across from the Hunter College campus, and hungry for something quick from the grill. Your conviction that the sentencing would be little more than a formality—the obligatory closing of the legal books—was sufficiently strong so that you had not even thought to inquire. Indeed, when Joe asked if you had heard about the players, you still failed to make the connection.

"Which players?" you asked.

"Which players do you think? The guys from City and LIU, the dumpers."

"No, what about them?"

"Four of them were sent to jail," he said.

"Are you serious?"

"Sure, I'm serious," Joe said. "You guys better watch it."

"Which four?" you asked him.

"I don't know," he said, "they didn't say."

"Who didn't say? Where did you hear it?" you wanted to know.

"Where did I hear it? The judge called me up. I heard it on the radio, where do you think I heard it?"

"Was Roman one of the four?" you asked.

"I just told you I don't know. All I heard was Eddie Gard and that Mafia guy who was fixing all the games."

"Sollazzo?"

"Yeah, Sollazzo. They named Sollazzo and Gard, but they didn't say which players."

So now the matter was open to speculation. Since as a group you probably were more familiar than most with the details of the case, you did not balk at the opportunity to play judge. If four players had been given jail terms, then Schaff was certain to be among them, because, for a time at least, he had worked directly for Sollazzo and Gard. Beyond Schaff, there was a difference of opinion, but the consensus settled on Bigos and Mager, since they had been the initial contacts for LIU and City. But no agreement could be reached on a fourth player. If the sentences were contrary to every legal precedent, you reasoned, then the intent of the judge must have been to establish a new precedent, a judicial guideline for players who even now might harbor a taste for some quick, easy money. But no one could think of a fourth player who seemed to be more intimately involved than the others.

"Are you sure Gard was not one of the four?" you asked.

Joe shook his head. "Four besides Gard. You guys just better be careful," he said. "They don't serve hamburgers like these in jail."

On the way home, you found yourself hoping that the fourth was not Ed Roman. He was the only one of the players you knew at all. You did not know him very well, but you had spoken with him on occasion, you had played on the same concrete court more than once, and if a fundamental decency of nature could serve as ballast against imprisonment, then Ed Roman did not belong in jail. For though he was a neighborhood hero of sorts, he had never learned to act the part. Even through the days of his greatest triumphs, he was humble and unassuming, even appearing at times embarrassed by a role that had claimed him without his asking.

You recalled a three-man game in which Roman was playing pivot on the opposing team. You had beaten your man on a drive to the basket and Roman slid off to pick you up. His arm was extended high over your head when you went up for the shot, but he didn't move it. He held it high but steady as you laid the ball up underneath, and you knew that he could have slammed it to the ground if he had chosen, but he did not wish to claim his natural advantage. You had earned the shot, he felt, and if you would not be intimidated by his presence, he would let you take it.

You thought of that on your way home, and later that evening you learned that Roman was not among those headed for jail; neither was Bigos or Mager. Judge Streit, it turned out, had a surprise or two in store. He had brought to his deliberations a set of criteria that you had not even begun to contemplate, and he was not quick to make it known. The judge had prepared for the occasion a statement of some ten thousand words which was more than an hour in the reading, and if the courtroom has often served as stage for some of the very best moments of theater, this day would not be the exception. For Judge Streit was more than halfway through his remarks before offering even the barest suggestion of what the disposition of the case might be. It was an excellent piece of theater—part soliloquy and part monologue, moral incantations spiked with forebodings of doom, excursions into sociology mixed with the hard coin of legal tender—the judge's words unwinding as if from a spool, flowing in the direction of that solemn moment in a packed auditorium when no one in the crowd feels the need to clear his throat.

Streit's opening remarks encouraged the prospect that the players would be dealt with mainly as victims—certainly no worse than accomplices—of academic corruption. For he began by sketching a detailed picture of transgressions and abuses that far exceeded a frivolous tampering with the amateur code. It was a panoramic but carefully documented chronicle of commercialization, subsidization, and recruitment, and it was not merely rhetoric. The judge had done his homework. He told of college administrations doctoring high school transcripts, of coaches openly bidding for the services of athletes; he recounted offers of gifts and money, wages paid for bogus jobs, a litany of offenses that included forgery, exploitation, bribery, and fraud. Streit cited the ways.

LeRoy Smith had been given a scholarship consisting of room, board, twenty dollars a week in meal money, and a job at which he did not have to work. His salary fluctuated with the quality of his performance on the court.

Sherman White, who had been widely scouted, was turned down by Duquesne for scholastic deficiency, had withdrawn after one semester at Villanova because of poor grades, and was given a scholarship by LIU. In his senior year, his program included courses in music seminar, oil painting, rhythm and dance, public speaking, and physical education.

Dolph Bigos and Dick Feurtado had received tryouts at the LIU gym before they were permitted to enter the university. Later, when Feurtado complained that he was not being properly compensated, his mother was sent twenty dollars a week by the athletic department.

Eddie Gard also was given a tryout while still in high school, and he was recruited again by Clair Bee when they were both stationed at the same Merchant Marine base during World War II. Gard's grades were below requirements, and after he was discharged he was sent to a prep school with all expenses paid, and then given a scholarship to LIU.

Connie Schaff was sent to the same prep school, Brooklyn Academy, by NYU, with his expenses paid by an alumnus or sponsor of the university. He was absent twenty-six days, failed to compile a passing average, and after one semester NYU gave him a scholarship.

Al Roth and Herb Cohen had entered City College on the strength of records that indicated "deliberate fraud and probable forgery." Their high school transcripts had been altered to make them eligible to take the entrance examination, and their exam papers apparently had been upgraded to meet City's requirements.

If Streit's revelations raised a few eyebrows, only the uninitiate might have been truly shocked. It was a distillation that served mainly to confirm suspicions long held in both basketball and gambling circles. LIU, clearly, was more than the equal of its reputation, for the practices cited by the judge did not surface as deviations, but rather as part of a policy that seemed to be lodged at the heart of the university's intent. In effect, LIU functioned less as a university than a corporation which recruited key personnel, paid a hair's worth more than its competitors, and even offered training courses for those who were short of qualification. It was a circumstance that did not go unnoticed by Streit, and Clair Bee was his most ready target. He noted that Bee's salary had risen by 300 percent between 1941 and 1950, and that he had been advanced to a full professorship and appointed vice-president of the university.

"Although the gross receipts at LIU for basketball for the year 1949 were thirty-eight thousand dollars," Streit said, Bee's " 'records' show that the college 'lost' twenty-four thousand dollars on basketball that year. He computed the loss by charging against income thirty to forty scholarships at a thousand dollars each, his salary, the salaries of two assistants, equipment, traveling expenses, and publicity. He considered basketball just a business venture but well worth the investment because it gave prestige and publicity to the school. In brief, all of the players entrusted to the care of LIU were openly exploited in behalf of Mr. Bee and the university."

LIU, of course, did not sire the system it practiced. Conceivably, it might have appeared the very model of temperance and restraint when compared with some of the larger sports emporiums in the South and Midwest. Streit knew that, and he offered up a bill of particulars regarding such schools as Michigan, Bradley, Ohio State, Oklahoma, and Kentucky that made even LIU seem a small-time operation. He then proceeded to an attack on the entire system of intercollegiate sports that was bitter and unsparing, and that fixed the locus of responsibility on college administrators, coaches, and alumni groups. "The acts of these defendants," he said, turning back to the players, "are merely the symptoms of the disease."

But if the judge's remarks nourished the promise of clemency toward the players, it was a mood that was soon dispelled. The first indication that things might not go easily came when the court barred all female relatives of the defendants from the eleventh-floor courtroom "to prevent any possible hysterical outburst." Since Sollazzo was not the likely object of great hysteria, and since Gard had already spent some time in jail, one had cause to infer that at least some of the players were due for prison terms.

Streit began the ritual of sentencing with Sollazzo. He took several minutes to recount Sollazzo's long criminal record and to detail the charges against him. Then, describing him as a "cool, calculating and cunning weasel, who preys on the gullible and unsuspecting," he sentenced the defendant to eight to sixteen years in State Prison.

Next he turned his attention to Gard. "If you were not so cooperative," he told Gard, "your sentence would be the same as Sollazzo's." But Gard, after all, had been the pivot of the state's case. So valuable was the information he had to offer, and so sensitive, that he had been held in protective custody for ten weeks. Now, for his "inestimable aid" in sharing what he knew with the district attorney's office, he was given an indefinite term of up to three years, with credit to be given for the time he had already served.

So now it came down to the players. One by one, they were summoned before the bench to confront the judge as he spoke briefly of their past, reciting in some detail their assets and debits, and weighing one side against the other as if the fate of each player would be decided on a balance sheet that could tabulate and measure the very substance of his life.

Bigos was the first to be called, and Streit began by listing his credits. "His early life," he said, "was without untoward incidents," and he noted in particular that Bigos had seen action in the South Pacific during World War II and had earned five battle stars, two Bronze Stars, and a Combat Infantryman's Badge. Streit then proceeded to the debit side. "This defendant," he said, "admits participating in the dumping of seven games and attributes his moral seduction to the niggardly treatment accorded him by LIU. I don't place much credence in that. In my opinion, this defendant is guilty of a series of briberies without regard for his honor or the public interest. But I must take into consideration his excellent record with the U.S. Armed Forces." And then, the calculation made, the bottom line of the ledger came up in the black. "Sentence is therefore suspended."

The tabulation for Feurtado and Miller, also the owners of proud war records, proceeded along similar lines, with the same result. Then, apparently working his way first through the LIU players, the judge summoned LeRoy Smith. Smith was not a service veteran, but Streit was nonetheless able to find grounds for salvation. He pointed out that Smith's high school record was "uniformly excellent" and that he was "the son of industrious, law-abiding, God-fearing parents . . ." Smith was, the judge concluded, an accidental offender who was the tool of White and Gard. Sentence was suspended, but the case now took on a new cast. White had, in effect, been named an associate of Gard's, and he was not called to the bench for sentencing. For the time being, Streit was finished with the LIU players, and he proceeded next to call Norm Mager.

Mager, of course, was the first City player to become involved. He was the initial contact and bagman for Eli Kaye, and the judge took due note. He said Mager had "induced the defendant, Roth, to participate, who in turn, secured the defendant Cohen's agreement. Then he influenced his teammates, Roman and Dambrot." But Mager had, after all, served with honor during the war, and the judge, who even today displays an Americanism Award from the Veterans of Foreign Wars on the wall of his office, was not the one to put a veteran behind bars. "Mager," he said, "I should send you to jail, but it is only because of your service to your country that I am extending to you extreme clemency. Sentence is suspended."

With the pardoning of Mager, it would not have been extravagant to assume that the other City players would be similarly spared, particularly when the judge whipped through the cases of Dambrot, Cohen, Layne, and Roman with something approaching formal dispatch. But there he stopped. Neither Warner nor Roth was called to step forward. They, together with White and Schaff, were going to be sent to jail. For here was Judge Streit announcing that "now I come to the most distasteful part of my duty in connection with this tragic scandal." The remaining players, he said, "stand in a special position of guilt" and "by virtue of their evil conduct, are different from those whose sentences I have just suspended." For close to ten agonizing minutes, the judge detailed the case against the four he had decided to give prison terms before he finally summoned them to the bench.

White, he said, was responsible for drawing Smith into the scheme, and he had also helped to break down Layne's resistance. He noted, too, that White had appeared before the Juvenile Court in 1943 (at the age of fourteen), and was arrested once for petit larceny and twice for disorderly conduct in 1945. He said that White's "moral and ethical standards left much to be desired. With his limited judgment and insight," Streit continued, "he became greedy and glamor-struck and developed an insatiable lust for night clubs and the company of girls."

As for Warner, the judge disclosed that in 1945 he "was hailed to the Children's Court as a member of the Sabers, a Harlem hoodlum gang," for having quarreled with a member of another street gang. He also noted that Warner's high school record left much to be desired, and he concluded by saying he found the defendant to be "completely lacking in moral and ethical concepts."

Roth had no previous record, but Streit charged that it was he who originally persuaded Roman and Cohen to join the conspiracy. He said that Roth's "basketball success turned his head and he became vain, aggressive and greedy. His moral scruples deteriorated if he ever had any, and as I have indicated, he had insufficient grades to be admitted to City College . . ." Such was the case against Roth.

Schaff was singled out for his poor scholastic and attendance records. The judge said, too, that he was "lacking in the basic requirements of character which would entitle him to sympathy for deviation from the normal path."

Now, with the gristle of each player's life ground through the court and digested, Streit came to the expedient of his decision:

"For these many reasons and with great reluctance, I find that suspended sentences will not suffice for these four defendants. They may serve as a warning to other college athletes who may be tempted that they cannot break the ideals of American sport and then escape with a mere reprimand."

He sentenced White to a year, and Warner, Roth, and Schaff to six-month terms in the penitentiary.

That concluded what was, in its way, a bizarre proceeding. Streit had begun by offering into evidence every conceivable reason for pardoning the players. Their acts were "merely the symptoms of the disease," he had said. Yet he chose to become the first judge ever to send an amateur athlete to jail for the crime of fixing sports contests. By the time the scandal had run its course, twenty-two players from six colleges had been prosecuted in New York, but only four of them received jail terms. Even more curiously, of the principal contact men for each of the schools, only Schaff was sentenced to prison, and White, who had never worked directly for a gambler, received a longer term than would be given to at least six of the fixers.

Of course, the application of justice is necessarily an imprecise endeavor, and sentences for the same offense have been known to vary according to time, place, and jurisdiction. But all of the players prosecuted in New York, with the exception of Poppe and Byrnes, were sentenced in Judge Streit's court, thirteen of them on the same day, and yet it required a degree of insight and something of a mind for conjecture to begin to trace the judge's course.

Immediately prior to issuing the four jail sentences, Streit explained that he had devoted months to the study of each of the defendants, carefully considering their case histories, their records, and their activities. He had concluded that these four were different from the others "by virtue of their evil conduct," and this decision was reached by weighing four fundamental factors. The judge named them:

First, they "were not merely victims of temptation; they were corrupters of others."

Second, they were "mature young men, all over twenty-two years of age, who should have known the iniquity of their conduct."

Third, "their criminal acts were persistent, continuous and many."

Fourth, "they profited largely from their continued dishonesty, receiving from five hundred to fifteen hundred dollars per fixed game."

It was not an unreasonable set of premises on which to proceed, but it was difficult to know just how Streit had applied them. For on the basis of his own criteria, it appeared that the wrong players had been sent to jail.

White, who received the longest term, had hardly been the first to introduce the corruption of point shaving at LIU. He had been invited in by Bigos after the game with North Carolina State. Nor even was Bigos the first. Feurtado, Miller, and Lipman, whose sentence was suspended a month later, were all fixing games at LIU long before White had received a dime. In like fashion, it was Mager who, in the judge's own words, had induced Roth to participate, and Warner did not become involved until the following season. So the charge of being "corrupters of others" would seem to apply more to players who were freed than to those given jail terms.

As for being mature young men, beyond the age of twenty-two, more than half of the players who received suspended sentences were the senior of the four ordered to serve time. Bigos was twenty-six, Lipman was twenty-seven, and Mager, Feurtado, and Miller all were twenty-five. In fact, Roman was the only player not yet twenty-two.

If the number of fixed games and the amount of money received were critical in formulating judgment, it should have been noted that Bigos apparently had fixed more games and received more money than any of the others. Warner had been charged with only three offenses, fewer than five of the players and no more than three others. And Schaff, despite his efforts, had succeeded in fixing only one game and had received less bribe money than eight of the other players. Yet he received the same jail term as the two men who bribed him.

It was a mystifying pattern the judge wove, particularly if one tried to reach the same conclusion by applying his own standards of judgment. Of course, the judge had two rather distinct sets of standards, and the one he proclaimed was different from the one he applied. The maturity of the players, the sums of money they received, the number of games they fixed, their degree of involvement with gam-

blers, the roles they played in corrupting others were given consideration, but they were not the fundamental criteria on which judgment
was passed. White, Warner, Roth, and Schaff would not have received jail terms if they had been old enough for service during World
War II, or if they had proven to be more serious students, or if their
backgrounds and life styles had been better suited to the judge's taste.
Roth, in fact, had his sentence suspended when he announced his
intention to enter the armed forces. For the judge, apparently, did
not feel obliged to reach a decision based strictly on the merits of the
case. What took place in the courtroom that morning was less a
judicial proceeding than a rendering of final judgment, for its intent
was not to fit the punishment to the charge but rather to the mood
and manner by which the player had lived. Thus LeRoy Smith could
be spared, at least in part, because he was the son of industrious,
God-fearing parents. But Warner, who had grown up an orphan in
the steaming caldron of West Harlem, would be shown no mercy.
And so sentence was passed in the best of ancient traditions. The sins
of the fathers were visited upon the sons, and the fathers' credits—
their time spent in the service of the Lord—were taken to offer a
measure of grace. Judge Streit was not the one to ignore the prece-
dents of higher courts.

But then the judge was heir to a different time in America, perhaps
the very last of a generation whose roots were sunk in the rich soil
of proud glories and hard-earned conquests. For a man who had lived
through the thirties and forties might be trusted to know that the
sweetest of triumphs often grew from the seeds of the most profound
deprivation. Yes, the sons of the Depression knew the story well.
They had seen their country emerge from the deepest pits of despair
and, like a roused Goliath, answer the call of beating drums to cross
great oceans and march across strange lands, and finally raise its flag
atop high and distant summits. There seemed to be magic loose in
the land then; gold had been coined from burned-out ashes, and if
there ever was a time in the nation's history when the future of
America appeared wedded to the best hope and destiny of mankind
it was during those fine bright years of resurrection. Our fantasies and

illusions—culled from airy wisps of breeze and bubble—had somehow hardened into reality, and for a time it seemed possible that the very mythology of an age might be rewritten by the brave deeds of mortals who had dared to sip from the chalice of the gods.

So one did not have far to look to find true and proper heroes then, heroes still cut to the dimensions of fable and folklore, heroes who fought and heroes who toiled, heroes who strode the playing fields of America like the Greek gods of Homer and Aeschylus. They hit home runs that healed lame children, they scored touchdowns for orphans, and knocked out opponents in cold defiance of gamblers and hoods. They were heroes who were not merely athletes; they were invested with the power to cure, with the strength, the courage, and the unfailing goodness to bestow the gifts of the gods. And if the gifts they brought were sometimes gone too soon, there was always one still left in the box, and it was given freely. They gave to America the gift of hope.

Judge Streit well understood the stature of such heroes, and in his opening remarks he sometimes invoked terms that might have been better suited to Mount Olympus than to Madison Square Garden. He spoke of "the temple of amateur sport" and referred to the "worship" of sports heroes. Athletes, he said, become models for millions of youngsters throughout the nation, and whoever tampers with this tradition "undermines the faith of young Americans and shatters its ideals and belief in integrity and character."

Judge Streit indeed belonged to another time in America, to a fading age when the sultans of sport still lived like gods in the ageless imagination of the young.

> *Where have you gone, Joe DiMaggio?*
> *A nation turns its lonely eyes to you.*

And DiMaggio, the great DiMaggio, was indeed gone now. He had played his last game just a month earlier, and in a matter of three weeks he would announce to the world that he was leaving. But Judge Streit belonged to another time, and he did not know that Joltin' Joe had left and gone away.

PART
FIVE

17

For the most part, it was over now. Only nine months had passed since the first arrests were made in February, but it seemed to be much longer than that, for so much had changed. The world of basketball had long been very much its own—not unlike an independent republic, with its own laws, its own citizens, its capital and points of interest, its regional differences, its rites and devotions—and it had all changed now, quickly and forever. It was as if a revolution of the spirit had taken place, a cruel turning of the soul, which left the republic looking much the same to those outside it, but grotesquely transformed to one who knew it from within.

Of course, the realization did not come all at once. It grew upon you slowly, like the death of one who is close, whose loss is assimilated after the first shock, but then is felt even more sharply, more painfully, at times and places where you might expect to find him and must learn all over again that, no, your friend is still gone and will not be seen again, not even here.

So the true pain of it, the measure of the loss, was yet to be felt. It would come again a few weeks after the sentencing, with the opening of the new basketball season. There would still be college doubleheaders at Madison Square Garden, the marquee would still burn bright in the dusk, the court would still be lit, would still answer in hollow echo to the beating of the ball and the sound of sneakered feet, but it did not seem to belong to New York any longer. It seemed more the property of teams from Kansas and Kentucky, from Dayton, Ohio, and from Brigham Young in Utah, and La Salle in Philadelphia. St. John's was still there, of course, and so were NYU and Manhattan, but LIU and City were gone, and it was City that would truly be missed, for it had been the pride and property of New York alone. It was City that had given true flavor to the regional encounters, the match-ups between New York players and players from the Midwest and the Far West and the South, the collision of playing styles that reflected the subtle shadings of mood and disposition; size versus speed, power poised against the brittle weavings of finesse. It would not be that way again. St. John's was to play in the NCAA finals that season, but the game would be played not in the Garden, but in Seattle, which was as far from New York as the game could be taken. The NIT still was the exclusive property of New York, but some of the shine had been taken from it. The NCAA winner was considered the national champion, and no team would ever again have the chance to coin gold twice by winning them both. In fact, the NIT had already begun its descent into oblivion. Twenty-five years later it would be known as a losers' tournament, and it would be played in a half-empty Garden. But it did not take twenty-five years to know it. Even then, in the fall of 1951, the signs were already there to be read.

You think about it again during the 1952–53 season, while warming up in the City College gym. The City gym seems very large compared to your own, and the court somehow harder, less resilient to your step. The rims are tight and live, and you note that you will have to shoot cleanly here, looking only for net and not trusting too much to the shooter's bounce. But what is most vivid, the impression that would be remembered years later with the greatest clarity, was the sense, serene yet oppressive, of an era having passed, of time lost on the wind, some small part of youth eaten away and left strewn in sullen and forlorn places. If time had not taken its vengeance, you think, this might be the floor of Madison Square Garden under your feet, with its banked tiers up above the backboard, and that might still be Nat Holman sitting there at the end of the City bench as he had for the past thirty-two years. For Holman is gone now, and in his place is the youthful Dave Polansky.

It was not simply the passing of the baton that made Polansky basketball coach at City College, for Holman had become a late casualty of the scandal. Almost two years after his players were arrested and a full year after they were sentenced, Holman was suspended as head coach of City for "conduct unbecoming a teacher" and "neglect of duty." And now, the very proud Holman, who for most of his fifty-six years had worn the title of "Mr. Basketball," had just cut short a sabbatical in Madrid and returned home to "defend the reputation which took a lifetime to build."

The charges against Holman also embraced several other members of the athletic department, including Bobby Sand, the assistant coach; Frank Lloyd, chairman of the hygiene department; and Sam Winograd, faculty manager of athletics. But Holman, of course, was the focus of the proceedings. More than history, more even than legend, would need to be accounted for when Holman came to trial, because Holman represented something more than the sport of basketball. He was symbol to an earlier era and life style in New York, and if basketball was the nutrient of his life, it might as easily have been another sport or another profession. For it was not just his skill that set Holman apart, not just his precocious scoring ability or his instinctive grasp of every fine and hidden subtlety of the game; it was his style and his presence, his fierce and stubborn dignity, the invisible magic of a hard-edged pride that seemed to insist, right from the start, that it was something special to be Nat Holman, something that could not be compromised or traded upon.

In the twenties, when Holman played for the Original Celtics, the team traveled from city to city, playing four or five games a week, and some of the players were known, on occasion, to walk into an out-of-town gym, don the uniform of the local team, and pick up some extra money playing under an assumed name. But Holman would never use an alias; he would play under no name other than his own, and it was doubtless something more than an idle vanity. For Holman was just one generation this side of the Old World, and he perhaps had an intuition that one's name was not an arbitrary thing, it was not merely a label that was appended. Name, after all, was essence; it was the sacramental root to the truth of one's past.

Blacks of a later generation would act upon the same imperative. If name was essence, then to violate its truth was sacrilege, and the blacks of the sixties and seventies who renounced names like Clay and Alcindor in favor of Ali and Jabbar were seeking not to destroy their past but to reclaim it. They were seeking, in fact, a name, an identity that offered some clue to the shape of their beginnings, the intimation of a memory that might run back to the womb. Yes, whatever its origin, name was essence, and Holman understood that one did not give up one's name without destroying something in the seed.

But then Holman was a patrician of sorts. He was the son of Russian immigrant parents, and he had grown up in the tenement-stacked streets of New York's Lower East Side, but he was a patrician nonetheless. The studied elegance and formality of his manner, his fastidious attire, the care with which he chose his words and the precision with which he used them, the very bearing and mood of the man—gray-streaked hair parted slightly to the right of center, hazel eyes set like chipped fragments of marble in the finely cut contours of his face—spoke of walls hung with ivy and stately old mansions snuggled in the solemn slopes of New England propriety. It was a style that did not come to Holman entirely by chance. For the better part of ten years he had begun his day by listening to the morning lectures at Town Hall, his ear tuned less to the speaker's message than to the sound and rhythm of the spoken word. "Speech deserves the respect of using it as well as you can," he had said, and Holman learned to use it better than most. Standing before a banquet audience, he could evoke intimations of Harvard with his broad *a*'s and a soft broguish roll in the timbre of his voice. But in the gym, in the heat of a game, he often would revert to the rapid staccato that more nearly resembled the accents of his youth. Holman indeed was a curious composite. On the surface he wore a smooth veneer, a regal sheen that suggested the courtly poise of F. Scott Fitzgerald. But beneath the glitter was a core as hard and as tough as coiled hemp, as stark and unrelenting as the gray concrete of the streets which had claimed him.

Holman had learned to play basketball in the schoolyards of the Lower East Side, and by the time he was twelve years old he was competing against established neighborhood players. But he learned to compensate. He studied the game closely and decided that ball handling and movement were "the two most essential parts of basket-ball." He worked on those skills and refined them, and in a sense they became his monuments, because it was the patterned precision of clockwork movement that distinguished every team that Holman played for or coached. He earned his first measure of fame playing on a city championship team for Commerce High School, and then worked his way through the Savage School for Physical Education by playing professional basketball for six dollars a night. In 1919, at the age of twenty-three, he was appointed head coach at City College, and two years later he staked his claim on a slice of basketball mythology when he joined the Original Celtics. The Celtics played as many as 150 games a season, and over a nine-year span, playing on slippery dance floors and in badly lighted halls all over the country, they were able to win 96 percent of the 1,386 games they played. It was an exquisitely honed team, a team with balance and speed and stamina that seemed somehow to intuit every nuance of a game that was barely thirty years old. But according to Holman, it was the grace of pride that meant most to the Celtics. "Pride in ourselves," he said. "The stories you read about champions getting weary of winning are so much nonsense. No champion ever wins so many contests that he doesn't mind losing one."

It was just such pride, the pride in being Nat Holman, that brought him back to New York near the end of 1952. He was on a one-year sabbatical, and he would have been eligible for retirement at the end of the school year, but Holman had no mind to retire, not while under suspension by the Board of Higher Education. No, Nat Holman would not leave until he had completely cleared the name that thirty years earlier he had been too proud to change.

The charges against him were rather nebulous. The Board's Committee on Intercollegiate Basketball alleged in its report that Holman was "either familiar with many aspects of big-time basketball . . . or else was so naïve about matters involving his own job as to throw doubt on his fitness as a teacher." On precisely such grounds Holman, who had been at City for thirty-four years, was summarily suspended. The charges against Sand and Lloyd were somewhat better defined, but then action had already been taken against them. Together with Sam Winograd, they had been relieved of all duties connected with the athletic department "in line with [City's] policy of revamping and modifying [its] athletic program." Lloyd and Winograd were given teaching assignments, and Sand took a year's leave of absence. None of the three had appealed the action, and the matter doubtless would have rested there had not the Board of Higher Education chosen to assume a role of moral leadership. The Board, of course, was in a tenuous position, for it was the Board that sanctioned big-time basketball in New York City, that granted permission for its teams to play in the Garden, that at least indirectly reaped some of the financial benefits that accrued from gate receipts. It was the Board that was responsible for policing the activities of its schools, and that approved the budget within which athletic programs were conducted. Holman, in fact, accused the Board of using him as a "scapegoat" in trying to "cover its own policy delinquencies over the past eight years."

Nonetheless, the Board appointed a three-man trial committee to hear the case, and what followed was a proceeding that might yet endure as a landmark in the double-jointed administration of justice. The trial occupied eighteen days but covered a period of almost six months, from May to November 1953. The prosecution took its job seriously. Among the witnesses it called was a former City College student who was taken off a troop ship on the way to Korea and brought back to New York to testify. After the trial ended, close to another three months passed before the three-man committee rendered its judgment. Holman was cleared of all charges by a vote of two to one, and Sand was found guilty by all three members. Lloyd had resigned when the trial opened, and charges against him had been dropped. The committee recommended that Holman be reinstated with back pay and that Sand be suspended for one year and then reassigned outside the department. But that was just the beginning of it. The committee sent its recommendation to the full Board, which required only one day of deliberation to reject the entire report of the three men it had appointed. In fact, the Board's fifteen voting members (six were not present) made a complete reversal, dismissing Holman and restoring Sand to faculty duties immediately. Among those who aided the Board in reaching its decision was Milton Mollen, the assistant corporation counsel, who had prosecuted the case. The Board heard no other witnesses, took no new testimony, introduced no additional evidence, and in a one-day hearing contravened the judgment of its own committee, which had studied the case for a period of nine months.

The Board's decision, however, was not peremptory. Holman was given the option of retiring and collecting his full pension, but he chose instead to appeal the dismissal to the State Education Commission. Arguments were heard on May 25, one year to the day since the trial had started, and three months later Holman was reinstated to the faculty with full back pay. In the fall, just before workouts started for the 1954–55 season, Holman was restored as head coach for his thirty-third season. Dave Polansky, who had replaced him during his two-year absence and who would finally succeed him when he retired in 1960, was named coach of the freshman team.

But now it is Polansky, not Holman, at the City College bench as the warm-up period ends with the sound of the buzzer. You walk slowly from the court, huddle briefly with the rest of the team, and then take your seat at the far end of the Hunter bench. You watch somewhat distractedly as the ball, a glistening orange satellite, goes up at center court and then hangs there for an instant against the bright lights of the gym, all motion frozen in a soundless tableau as ten uniformed players wait poised and tense for the ball to start its descent. Then, suddenly, as if a blister had burst, the court erupts in a blur of frenzied movement. Basketball must appear a chaotic game to the undisciplined eye, you think, because now, as you watch, there seems to be no form or pattern to what is taking place on the floor. The game is proceeding as any other, you know, the players moving and sliding in and out of constellations that are as familiar to you as the cut and weave of a coat to a tailor, but you do not recognize them, for the part of your mind that unscrambles what the eye sees is unprepared to do its work. It is focused elsewhere now, and all that filters through is a succession of sounds and sights—an occasional whoop from the crowd, the constant thudding and squeak of rubber against hardwood, the sound of a whistle, a buzzer, the sharp cries of voices calling "slide" or "pick," a rush of purple jerseys matched in step by white, lights blinking and flashing on the scoreboard—and all of it is seen and heard as if from inside an airless bubble, through the once familiar, now strange glare and cadence of a basketball court.

The sleeves of your sweat suit are slippery against the trouser legs as you lean forward on the bench, elbows on knees, chin cupped in the palm of your hand. You wear your warm-up jacket unbuttoned and the trouser zippers are left open at the ankles to indicate a state of readiness, but the call never comes, and the half ends, and now you are back in the locker room sucking the juice from an orange and waiting for the second half to begin. This is the City College locker room, the City College gym, you keep reminding yourself, and try as you might you cannot keep the past from insinuating itself into the present. For something appears to be truly ending now, you cannot say what exactly, perhaps something that had already ended but whose passing you were not yet ready to concede. You think now of schoolyard games long forgotten, of trips through summer evenings with a ball tucked under your arm, and nighttime rides on double-decker buses. You think of people and places that had already begun to wash from memory, of childhood friends who had slipped away, a store that had closed, a face that had vanished, a youth who died too soon. You cannot tell where it is coming from or what it all means. Perhaps time must be paid more dearly before the past will surrender its truth.

Back on the court now, you think of Roman and of Warner and Layne and Roth. You remember that March night in the Garden against Bradley, and the Sunday morning in Nat's poolroom, where you first heard the news. How long ago it all seems now, and how suddenly it has changed, and yet how quickly and effortlessly the time has passed. The players who had been sent to prison have all served their sentences. They are free now to begin retrieving the pieces, to try to divine some form and shape for the remnants that remain. Yes, you think now of the players who had gone to jail, and for some reason it is Sherman White who occupies the forefront of your thoughts. Perhaps it is because his term was the longest, or because he was by far the best of them and therefore stood to lose the most, but now, even as the second half is beginning, you remember Sherman White being taken into custody, towering above the arresting officer by the better part of a foot. The officer, a detective, had tried to offer White the consolation of small talk.

"Everyone gambles," the detective said.

"Sure," said White, "but no one gambled higher than me."

Almost two years had passed since then, but the case still had not been marked closed. For most of the past year, the grand jury had been hearing testimony on one last piece of business. It involved three players on the Kentucky team that had succeeded the Beard-Groza NCAA champions of 1949, the team that City had beaten so badly in the NIT but that had gone on to win its own NCAA title a year later, the Kentucky team led by All-American Bill Spivey. That team, the indications were, had been fixing games for two seasons in field houses all over the South and Midwest. Inquiries were being conducted in thirteen states, and Spivey, Walter Hirsch, and Jim Line were brought to New York for questioning. Hirsch, who had been graduated and was serving in the Army, and Line, who was assistant coach to Adolph Rupp, made their admissions to the grand jury. They were clear of criminal charges, because none of the games had been played in New York, but Spivey was playing his senior year at Kentucky, and with the prospects of a professional career that might be the equal of any in the NBA, he denied any complicity in point shaving. It was too late though. Line had told the grand jury that he had acted as intermediary between the fixers and Spivey and Hirsch. Hirsch had testified that Spivey, then a lowerclassman, had come to him and asked to be included in the fixes. Spivey's denials resulted in a perjury indictment and a two-week trial that ended with a hung jury. The indictment finally was dismissed, but the inquiry had already taken its effect. Adolph Rupp was suspended by the Southeastern Conference for a year, and Kentucky canceled its 1952–53 basketball schedule. The NBA ordered Spivey's name kept off the 1953 draft roster and barred him permanently. Seven years later, Spivey filed an unsuccessful suit against the NBA, charging he was blacklisted and asking $820,000 in damages. He was nearly thirty years old at the time, and he was averaging thirty-two points a game for the Baltimore team in the Eastern League.

Spivey would have been the NBA's first seven-foot center. He had become the dominant force in college basketball, the leader of the national champions. He had matured greatly in two years, acquired some polish and poise, learned to control his seven-foot body without its getting in his way. He was a different player now from the one you remembered going against Ed Roman in the 1950 NIT. Roman had given away half a foot that night and yet seemed to orchestrate Spivey's every movement. He held the bigger man to three shots in the first half, taking away floor position, fronting him, using his bulk and his brain to move Spivey outside, away from the basket where distance would serve as the best defense.

So now your thoughts turn back to Roman, and you remember matching shots with him in the schoolyard one afternoon, Roman flicking the ball from off his right shoulder, his touch as light and as soft as a breeze, and you trying to keep pace, pushing off from in front of your chest, the ball ticking off from the inside of your right forefinger in high looping arcs aimed at dead center of the cordless rim. Roman would grin casually, good-naturedly, as the ball fell through, offering words of praise when you made two or three in a row. You are lost deep in such thoughts, your mind swirling in reveries of recent events that seem to have happened very long ago.

But now you hear your name being called. It is called again and the coach is up off the bench, looking down in your direction and motioning toward the court. You look up at the clock. There are less than two minutes to play, and your team is hopelessly behind. You remove your sweat suit and hurry to the scorer's table. You give your name and the name of the man you are to replace, and then you kneel and wait and you watch as the clock winds down, the last seconds slipping dead into the past until the buzzer sounds and the game is ended and you are left there, alone and waiting, like a man on a railroad platform watching his train leave the station.

You are in haste to leave now. There is no need to shower, and you dress quickly, stuff your sneakers and purple road uniform into a carrying bag, and head for the subway. You know now that you are doing this all for the last time, that you are finished with varsity basketball. Of course, no one is ready to believe you. It is late Saturday night and those you tell are certain you will have changed your mind long before Monday morning, but you know it is over now. There are no factors to consider, no judgments to weigh, no assessments to be made of advantages lost or gained. There is just the sense that it has come to an end, for whatever complex of reasons you might never know, and that it is not, after all, of very great importance.

On Monday morning you would go to the coach's office. You would tell him that you were not getting much playing time, that the practice schedule interfered with your studies, that your grades had suffered. You would thank him for past favors, wish him well, and take your leave.

What you told him, of course, was true in every instance. Sound and reasonable explanations were never in short supply; it was just that they never explained very much. For you knew that you had thought of all the reasons after the decision had been irrevocably made. But then that made the explanations all the more necessary, for who would be ready to believe that you knew a thing had ended when each new moment already seemed to be a part of the past?

By the time the grand jury was dismissed it had heard testimony implicating thirty-two players in the fixing of eighty-six games from 1947 to 1950. Twenty of the players and fourteen men charged with bribing them had been indicted and convicted. What had begun as a New York City scandal, with Madison Square Garden its center, had spread across the nation. Games had been fixed in at least twenty-three cities in seventeen states, most of them in local gyms and field houses.

The numbers, of course, could not begin to offer proper scope. Since New York was the only city to conduct an investigation, one was left to speculate on what might yet lie uncovered in the heartland. If games had been rigged in more than one third of the states in the Union, was it really conceivable that only seven college teams were involved? If a New York grand jury turned up evidence on the fixing of eighty-six games in four seasons—an average of more than twenty a year—was it unlikely that a nationwide investigation might have found the true figure to be several times higher? And what of the years prior to 1947, the years when Jackie Goldsmith was building a reputation at LIU? Had not four Brooklyn College players been arrested as early as 1945? There were those who would tell you that more games were fixed between 1942 and 1946 than in the four years that followed. There were stories to be told of games in which both teams had agreed to dump for opposing gambling interests. Others cited instances in which players on the same team had been paid to go in opposite directions—one group trying to exceed the spread, the other working to stay below it. The investigation of the New York grand jury was, in all likelihood, no more than the equivalent of the first incision in exploratory surgery. One would never learn at what depth lay the seed, or how far it had traveled, or when it had taken root. And in a sense it did not matter. The measure of what had occurred could not be found in numbers. One knew only that college basketball was the most corrupt team sport in America, had been for perhaps the past ten years, and indeed might yet be, for who was there certain enough to give assurance that point shaving had ended in 1951?

Just three months after he was restored as head coach at City College, Nat Holman warned that we might not yet have seen the end of college basketball scandals. He told a meeting of the New Jersey Sports Writers Association that there was as much gambling on basketball in 1954 as there had ever been, and that "some gambler somewhere is going to approach a kid one of these days, and we'll have another dirty mess on our hands."

As it turned out, Holman's words were prophetic.

It happened not many years later; ten years and one month, to the very day, after the first scandal erupted. Two Bronx gamblers— well-known alumni of the Creston schoolyard, notables-in-residence at the Bickford's cafeteria on the corner of 188th Street and the Grand Concourse—were arrested for bribing basketball players at Seton Hall University and the University of Connecticut. Even before you saw the headline, you recognized the faces, the two one-column "head shots" on the front page of *The New York Times*. You knew one of them very well. You had grown up in the same neighborhood, played in the same street games, shared a wooden bench in the bleachers of Yankee Stadium. The other was known to you only by face. His name struck no chord of recollection, for you had known him over the years only by the Runyonesque pseudonym of Joe Jalop. He was the neighborhood bookmaker. So right from the start, you suspected that this was something that could grow very large, because neither of these two was a likely candidate for leadership of a nationwide consortium of fixers. And that was what the district attorney said was involved.

The new scandal broke very slowly, each new revelation spaced across months that finally stretched into years. First it spread south, and then back to New York, from where it worked its way west across the breadth of the country—Ohio, Michigan, Illinois, Iowa, until it finally reached the Pacific Coast. It spread that way for more than a year, an epidemic reluctant to peak, and it all came very slowly. More than a month passed before it became known that eight more players were involved at five other colleges—St. Joseph's, La Salle, the University of Tennessee, Mississippi State, the University of North Carolina. Then, weeks later, the taint reached North Carolina State; another few weeks and it came back home to St. John's, NYU, and Brooklyn College; almost another month and it was Columbia, Bradley, Dayton, the University of Iowa, Bowling Green, the universities of Detroit and Oregon. It seemed to have no end. After almost two years the tally showed that at least fifty players from twenty-seven colleges had been involved in fixing games in fifty-one cities and twenty-two states. There were other players and former players who had acted as go-betweens, still others who had declined bribes but failed to report them. By every measure it was a scandal more than twice the size of the first. It was next to impossible to calculate the number of games that had been fixed or tampered with, and the coast-to-coast network involved literally dozens of gamblers.

For many months, for more than a year in fact, the DA's office had been looking for a single point of connection, a central figure who would fit the standard police description of "mastermind" or "master fixer" or "Mr. Big." It was known that they were looking for such a man and the newspapers referred to him regularly as "Mr. X." But the district attorney had chosen his candidate some time ago and had him under close surveillance for perhaps two years.

On March 16, 1961, the day before the first two gamblers were seized, Jack Molinas took a plane to Washington, D.C. He had been invited to give a speech on "The Integrity of Basketball." On the same plane was a detective from Hogan's office. Molinas, who was an attorney, recognized him. He was not surprised to find him there. He had known for more than a year that he was being watched. He suspected that his phone was tapped. He knew that the DA's office referred to him as "the Spaniard," a reference no doubt to his Sephardic appearance—the olive complexion, the dark eyes and hair, the pronounced, somewhat elongated features of his pleasant, near-to-handsome face. It did not seem to trouble Molinas. Even after his associates were arrested and it appeared obvious that some of them, at least, had something to say, he remained cool and indifferent. He acknowledged that he wagered, and often won, large sums on basketball games. He said he was privy to information that gave him a gambler's edge. But he insisted that he knew nothing of the fixing of games and gave every indication that he had no grounds for concern. That he was under suspicion, that he was being followed, that his phone might be tapped, appeared only to amuse him.

"You could chill a bottle of beer with his blood," one gambler said of Molinas. But another, one who was as close to him as any, took a different view. "Cold-blooded, nothing," he said. "He's scared. He always was scared. He always was scared stiff, but he hid it."

Conflicting opinions were no surprise when it came to Molinas. He had always been a patchwork of the most strident contradictions—brilliant but bizarre; an intense competitor who rarely seemed pained by defeat; a free, gregarious, even frivolous spirit that nonetheless gave hint of a distant and uncertain isolation. He was an inordinately complex man, as difficult to comprehend as the mood of the Sphinx, and yet there was an aspect to his nature that was so basic, so fundamentally simple and precise, as to suggest a translucent rent in the darkness through which one might yet hope to see to the heart of the riddle.

From the start, he had known the uneasy attraction that the

middle class felt for underworld connections, the tantalizing flirtation with powers dark and mysterious that danced at the shores of the deeps. His first exposure came rather early. As a youngster, in the Coney Island section of Brooklyn, he was known to spend idle hours around a local bar and grill that was owned and operated by his parents and which was said to be a lure for gamblers and racketeers. When he was in his teens, the family moved to the then somewhat fashionable Grand Concourse in the West Bronx, just blocks from the Creston schoolyard. Creston, at the time, was known to breed basketball players and gamblers in approximately equal quantity, and Molinas held better than fair credentials in both fraternities. He was a gifted schoolyard player, an early candidate for All-America at Columbia, and it was no secret that he was given to placing an occasional bet on a sporting event. So Molinas was something of a local celebrity at Creston and a ready subject for speculation as well, for he seemed to be governed by a nameless device, an instrument of nullification that ground against the very best he had in him.

In the schoolyard, he would go one-on-one against Bernie Grant, and if the games were invariably closer than they should have been it was not Molinas's charity that offered the stake. Grant's skills, of course, were considerable, and he played with an intensity that seemed to cut the air around him, but still, he should have been no match for Molinas. He was almost a foot shorter, more than fifty pounds lighter; he did not possess the sheer physical gifts of Molinas, the practiced grace, the finely tuned motor discipline that one acquires on big-time courts. But Grant would win more than his share of the games because there was something in him that was terrified of losing, and in equal measure there was in Molinas a quality that suggested a fear of winning too often. It was as if Molinas lived with the foreboding that every success would cost its price, that there was an iron law in nature which insisted that for every deed that plucked moondust from the heavens, a bounty must be left for ransom at the steps of the charnel house. Whatever his degree of gain, Molinas could be trusted always to pay it back with interest.

At the end of his sophomore season, on his way to setting every scoring record at Columbia, he was suspended for hurling a glass from a dormitory window. In 1953 he was the first-round draft pick of the Fort Wayne Pistons, was named to play forward in the NBA All-Star game in his rookie season, and before the season was over he was suspended and then barred for life for betting on his own team. He turned to studying law at Brooklyn College, and at about the same time he was earning his law degree he began fixing basketball games on a nationwide scale, was disbarred and finally sentenced to ten to fifteen years in Attica State Prison. Even while in prison, Molinas continued to play across the checkerboard of his fortune. He was known as a shrewd investor, and during the four years he spent behind bars he was said to have amassed a large sum of money speculating in the stock market.

In November 1965, a little more than a year since he had begun serving his sentence, Molinas was secretly moved to Manhattan City Prison—the Tombs—where, indications were, he began a lengthy dialogue with the district attorney's office. It was widely presumed that in exchange for an early parole Molinas supplied the information that was necessary to break a massive race-fixing scandal at three metropolitan harness tracks. For a while rumors circulated that Molinas might be marked for death if he were released from prison. It was not the first time he had been the subject of such conjecture. About five years earlier, the word had spread that big-time gamblers had a contract out for Molinas, but he escaped, apparently, with only a beating and a broken finger. His parole came in 1968, and two years later he moved to California, where he became involved in a variety of ventures, ranging from partnership in a fur business, to dealings in pornography, to a scheme for purchasing the assets of firms facing expropriation overseas. He lived, as was his wont, in the best and highest of style. He drove big cars, traveled with expensive-looking women, and resided in a resplendent, rambling house in the Hollywood Hills. But there were those who said that the small fortune he had accumulated was at least equaled by a spectrum of very large debts. And his trouble with the law was not over. In 1973 he was arrested for shipping pornographic films interstate. The case never came to trial. Early one summer morning in 1975, Molinas was shot to death gangland style, a bullet fired through the back of his head while he stood with a lady friend appraising the view from his own backyard. His life ended as abruptly as his careers in basketball and law. But then Molinas was a man who courted quick endings.

The news of Molinas's death was carried in barely three inches of type at the bottom of the obit page. A more comprehensive account would be given almost a full column the following day, most of it filled with speculation on the motive of his assassin. There was no shortage of possibilities. Molinas's life had been a network of loose connections that ran through the conduits of palaces and dungeons, wired to the sockets of every dark room where money changed hands quickly and life found its pulse on the turn of a card. For what truly marked a gambler was not his devotion to winning, but an indifference to it, the unformed conviction that life was lived best when precise measure could be given to the cast and tone of one's changing fortune. There was little ambiguity in the life of a gambler. He was not obliged to contemplate the dimensions of success or failure. He knew. Each day, his life dictated, he must choose either one side or the other, and place his bet, and at day's end the wisdom of his choice could be calculated in the unambiguous precision of number. He would always know whether he was a step closer to salvation or that much nearer the steeps of the damned.

Yes, it was even conceivable that every true gambler was at bottom a fundamentalist. For was not the soul of fundamentalism forged in the wish to resolve all ambiguities? Since one could not share common ground with both Jehovah and Satan, went the catechism, then each act must be given definition in favor of either one or the other. And the promise of salvation lay in one's willingness, perhaps, to make a final choice, to risk one's spiritual capital on a leap across the mouth of the abyss. The heart of every gambler was buried deep in the soil of just such sorcery. It was not the tables of profit and loss that held the lure, but rather the slim sweet chance of laying a stake at destiny's door. Of course, the prospect of such sweets was not the purchase of the casual bettor. One would have to gamble high, he would have to be ready to lose far more than the promise of his gain. But then no one ever gambled higher than Molinas; not even Sherman White.

The prison term given to Jack Molinas was the stiffest ever handed a first-time offender under the sports bribery law. What made it even more remarkable was that the other sentences in the case were invariably lighter than they had been in the fifties. More than half of the gamblers charged with bribery or conspiracy had their sentences suspended. Others were given no more than probationary terms. At least one was let off with a fine no larger than the sum he might have wagered on a basketball game. The treatment of the players was commensurately lenient. They did not go to jail; indeed, they were not even prosecuted. District Attorney Hogan granted the players immunity in exchange for the evidence they could present to the grand jury. At the outset, Hogan even declined to identify the players, on the grounds that it would damage his case. Nowhere was there heard the echoes of the fifties—the righteous declamations, the moralizing pronouncements, the rhetoric about destroying the ideals of the young. It was as if all capacity for indignation had been squandered ten years earlier, washed and cleansed on the reefs of a harder reality.

Even in the colleges the reaction was random. If twenty-seven schools were in some degree involved, not half a dozen felt obliged to impose immediate sanctions. The response at St. John's, which had escaped the first time, was utter indifference. Its president, the Very Reverend John Flynn, promptly announced that the school "does not intend to de-emphasize basketball or any other sport of collegiate competition." It was a forthright statement by the Reverend, and if other college presidents were less candid, they offered little reason to believe that they felt much different. Seven of the colleges, in fact—St. John's and NYU included—fielded teams in the NIT or NCAA tournament the very next season. Illusion might die slowly, but it dies only once, and the world of college basketball was conceivably immune now to the breath of scandal.

Obviously, the harsh penalties dished out in the fifties had had no effect at all. All the talk about setting an example ("They may serve as a warning to other college athletes who may be tempted that they cannot break the ideals of American sport and then escape with a mere reprimand," Judge Streit had said) had meant nothing. The fixing of games had started again (if indeed it ever had ended) as early as 1957, no more than six years later, and by every indication the job of recruiting players had, if anything, become less arduous. It was as if the first scandal had given sanction to the next, in the way that any crime—no matter how grave, or how formidable the risk—grows less remote from conscience once the consequences are no longer unknown. Yes, precedent offered sanction; it was a principle on which a new behaviorism might yet be founded.

So the players of the sixties, in a curious, an almost perverse way, had profited from the lessons of the fifties. For they were dealt with, in the argot of law enforcement, more as accomplices than as perpetrators. They had not, after all, sullied the sport of basketball; by 1961, the sheen was already ten years gone. No, they could not be punished in like manner, the reasoning might have gone, they could not be sent to jail for destroying ideals that were already dead. For who would be left to mourn?

It was the scandal of the fifties that contained the dramatic content, that had torn pages from legend, and exposed college basketball as a game of intricate beauty that had nonetheless been fitted to the wheels of a slot machine. The improprieties of the sixties would soon be looked upon as little more than an aftermath, quickly forgotten and buried beneath the debris of memory. Ask the man at your elbow some night if he remembers the basketball fixes and buy a drink for the first who offers the names of Art Hicks or Hank Gunter or Ray Paprocky before he thinks to mention Sherman White or Ed Warner. See how many recall that St. John's or Seton Hall were ever involved in point shaving. *The Modern Encyclopedia of Basketball*, as complete and weighty a tome as exists on the sport, devotes an entire section of some three thousand words to the fifties scandal, but gives no more than two sentences, parenthetical in scope, to the sixties affair, which it says "did not involve as many teams, nor was it as far reaching . . ." Just so quickly is history lost to recollection, for it is the effect of an event, not the fact, that leaves its mark upon the past.

The only fate shared by the players of the two decades was that none of them would ever make his living playing professional basketball. Many of the players, particularly those from the fifties, played for a time in the Eastern League or the old American Basketball League. The ABL, which in the twenties was adorned by the Original Celtics, had disbanded in 1929, was revived in 1933, and in 1952 was finally torn apart and put out of business in a controversy over the signing of players involved in the scandal. But the Eastern League welcomed them. The Eastern League is a weekend circuit, as old as 1909, where players perform on Saturday and Sunday for fees ranging from thirty-five to two hundred dollars for the two games. It is a league composed principally of teams from small Pennsylvania mill towns such as Reading, Allentown, and Wilkes-Barre, which often play before audiences that can be counted in the hundreds. It is small-time basketball, largely a repository for marginal players who had not quite made it in the NBA, who are hanging on, staying in shape, looking perhaps for one more chance at the big time.

How remote it must have seemed to the likes of White and Warner and Roman! How gloomy the prospect of the poorly lighted courts, the small gyms with their makeshift bleachers, the piddling crowds of mine workers looking for a night out; how far from the thumping sounds and magical glare of the Garden on game nights, the crowds bursting at the outer reaches, the big, sophisticated yet wildly frenetic New York crowds, connoisseurs of rhythm and movement whose palates had been cultivated on concrete courts. Who was there to watch them now, and what was there to win? The mood must have been as depressing as that in a roadside gin mill where the piano-bar is played by a virtuoso who in better days had known the stage of Carnegie Hall.

And yet many of them stayed on for years. Twenty-five years later one was told that Sherman White, long past his fortieth year, was still playing in the Eastern League. You would think then of something Tubby Raskin, the coach of the 1945 Brooklyn College team, had said shortly after the City and LIU players were arrested.

"I'm not saying these boys didn't do wrong," Raskin said. "I'm not even saying they don't deserve punishment. All I'm asking is who is to decide the extent of that punishment? And after that who will force society to accept them as normal individuals without a stigma?"

The answer, of course, was no one. The road back would be tortuous and slow, but still it was there to be taken. In the end— except for having forfeited their basketball careers—most of the players very likely fared no worse than they might have. Almost all of the City players returned to college and obtained their degrees. Roman, in fact, studied for his doctorate while working as a teacher and counselor of emotionally disturbed children in the New York City school system. Dambrot completed his work at the Columbia School of Dentistry and has been conducting his own practice in Forest Hills. Roth became an insurance agent and then went into the real estate business. For the past ten years, Warner has been running playground tournaments and working with youngsters in community programs. Layne, of course, came full circle. He earned a master's degree, became a teacher, a playground coach, an interim varsity coach at Queensborough Community College, and in 1974 was named head basketball coach at City College. All of the starting players on City's grand-slam team still reside in metropolitan New York. None of them lists his home phone in the telephone directory. The scars of the soul heal, but they never disappear.

Had the players been guilty of a more conventional offense—a crime against person or property; a stolen car, a burglary, a simple assault—redemption no doubt would have come more quickly, more completely, and with less pain. But they had trespassed instead against something far holier than property. They had tampered with childhood ideals, and who among us would not sooner surrender his wallet than his trust? So the price extracted would be great indeed, greater than the jail terms some of them served, greater even than the lost chance to play professional basketball. The steepest price of

• 235

all was that no one would ever forget. People who had never met them, who had never seen them play, who knew or cared nothing about the sport of basketball, would recognize their names and identify them as dumpers. Every chance meeting, every new acquaintance made at a cocktail party would introduce the possibility of questions they might not wish to answer. And they knew, of course, that it would never be otherwise, that they were serving an informal sentence which had no end. At a very young age, something hard and final had turned in their lives, and they would never be quite the same again. Yes, they were obliged, in a sense, to become somewhat different men. And if the scar they bore would never vanish, neither would it soon be offered for public display. It was next to impossible to find a player who was ready to discuss either the pain or the glory of his past. Interviews were turned down with even the most sympathetic correspondents. Yet there were some who would speak candidly (if not for the record) for an hour or more in explanation of why they did not wish to give an interview. They would provide insight and information sufficient for the prelude to a treatise, and you would understand that the desire for secrecy always resides next to the need for revelation. So one would listen, without benefit of a note, and give assurance that nothing said would ever find its way to print.

Of course, it is never possible to know to what degree, or in what ways, a man has changed, for the change occurs slowly, imperceptibly, and it is like watching the hands on a clock; the movement is invisible, but then suddenly the hour chimes, and you know that somehow, without your noticing, time has passed and it has gotten late. There are events that have just such power of transformation because their consequences can never be fully digested. Some residue always remains, some vital quivering center that alters one's focus, and because it is there every perception of the future will be somewhat different than it might have been.

Well, other changes were perhaps easier to measure. Certainly, college basketball would not be the same again, not in New York. In the years to come, one would speak of college basketball in the fifties and the way the Garden was lit to a glow for City–St. John's or

NYU–Notre Dame with the same sense of loss and nostalgia that brought recollection of the Friday-night fights or Maglie versus Newcombe at the old Polo Grounds. Now, national championships were decided in other cities—large and small—while the Garden stood empty and solemn above the hollow drone of Penn Station. It was as if a native product had been sold to export, shipped out and reproduced in such quantity and with such precision that after a time there were few to remember that it had once been yours. Of course, New York would continue to produce its share of the nation's basketball players, but the best of them would not remain in the city where they had learned to play the game. They would play out their high school terms and then slip away to schools in Wisconsin or California or South Carolina, and return home perhaps once a season for a game in the Garden. But their fame would be earned in strange cities and on foreign courts. They became migrants in much the fashion of professional athletes, and twenty-five years later you might find yourself watching the NCAA on television and rooting for Marquette to beat Indiana because Butch Lee and a few others had grown up in the streets and playgrounds of New York. And without really trying, you would summon forth that night, so many long years ago, when the streets of your neighborhood emptied out and the block was left vacant because City was ready to go against Bradley, and everything you knew or understood seemed to be part of the stake. You could not know then, of course, that you were seeing it that way for the last time, that no game would ever be quite that important to you again, and as the years passed you could not always be certain how much of what you felt now was contained in the event itself or what part of your loss could be measured by a bright devotion that had faded with the years.

At the time, in the early fifties, the loss seemed to be irrevocable and complete. The game itself had lost none of its charm, the slow easy magic was still there, the unspoken dialogues that weaved their way into patterns of mysterious beauty and ended in the symmetry of a ball passing silently through a hoop. But basketball had been something more than a game in the schoolyards of New York; it had been a language of sorts, a way of seeing the world and communicating what one felt about it, a metaphor through which one began to learn something, to divine perhaps some notion of what the future might finally require and how high a price one might be ready to pay. And it was that—some thin but firm relation to something larger than itself—that seemed to be gone then. And it was as if a shadow had been cast across the heart; a shadow deep as darkness and as cold and bleak as the midnight sun.

EPILOGUE

You had been away a long time and now, twenty years later, you felt an alien in streets that once were yours. The landmarks that told the story of your youth had either disappeared or tarnished. New ones had emerged, but they were the property of others and there seemed to be little left that might inform the present of the past. All change is, in its way, a form of betrayal, and you could feel its touch now, rising slowly from some deep well of resentment. You found yourself walking farther than you had intended, combing the pavements as if in search of lost treasures and hoping that some silent keeper of your youth had held its secret against the passing of the years.

It was an unplanned journey, taken a small piece at a time, and you were not alone. At your side was your teen-age son, grown now to within inches of your own height, his hands thrust inside the pockets of his windbreaker, his collar turned up against the lingering chill of early spring. His quick easy gait matched yours stride for stride, each step taken lightly, almost tentatively, as if walking a tightrope that stretched its way through the tunnel of time. The terrain was not altogether strange to him. You had, after all, regaled him with not a few tales over the years, evoking the past as best you recalled it, and he knew to keep an eye peeled for places like Nat's and the Dungeon pool hall, for Pop's candy store and Bickford's, but they were not to be found. They were all gone now, replaced by a supermarket, a wash-'n'-dry, a store that advertised apartments for rent. But if most of what you found reflected two decades' worth of evolution, Bickford's might be said to have undergone a metamorphosis. For the random site that had served as a gambling parlor for an entire generation had become one of the city's largest off-track betting offices. So now it was the city that collected the vigorish, and the justice of poetry seemed a part of the change. Twenty years later, the city of New York had seen fit to license a part of your youth.

Well, it was here that your chance voyage really began. Bickford's had been the northernmost outpost in that loosely defined network of blocks that you had called your neighborhood, and now, just a half block away, you were attracted by the sight of a cluster of men standing about like idle sentries whose presence betokened a changing of the guard. But as you drew closer, you could see that the guard had not changed at all. There were familiar faces in the group, faces that reached back across the years and called forth faded recollections from half your life ago. Yes, they were still there. They had remained amidst the debris and the boarded-up stores, as if left to keep a vigil in the twilight of a day that had no end. The times had changed, the neighborhood had changed, but they had not. They stayed on, ageless in their way, like the forgotten souvenirs of a time gone by.

They had lived through it all, but none of it had touched them. Through the coiled insanity of witchhunts and the soporific of the Eisenhower years, through the brief promise and glitter of the Age of Kennedy and the sudden agony of its passing, through ban-the-bomb and fallout shelters, through the marches and sit-ins and freedom rides, through the burning of cities and riots on campuses, through the protests and peace strikes, through the Age of Drugs and the Age of Hip, through bombings and invasions, through sieges and strife, through Johnson and Nixon; men walked on the moon and died in the jungles, draft cards were burned and blood spilled in the streets, Presidents were elected and appointed and resigned; for two decades the walls shuddered and the foundations shook, and none of it mattered. They watched the years pass, and they grew older, but they never changed.

So you walked by and then you paused, thinking to go back, to talk to one of them you had known particularly well, to ask what he had been doing these past twenty years, but you decided against it. The answer was clear enough, and what could either of you possibly say? You tried, as best you could, to explain to your son what you yourself did not fully understand. You could tell him only that life required that people change, that one was obliged always to move on and leave certain things behind, and that this was a relentless process that began at a very young age and never really ended. It was, after all, no small part of wisdom to recognize the moment when the next step must finally be taken, to know that to remain and try to hold on will cost a price no one can ever afford. And even as you understood its truth, you could not still the yearning you felt inside, that bitter heartsick yearning for something that had been stored with time and that can never be retrieved.

It was late in the day now, and the sun was at your eyes as you walked west along 188th Street and then turned left into streets that, even transformed, would always be more familiar to you, more inviting in their way, than any you would ever know. For each step seemed to summon something from the past: a face that was twelve years old, a name you could only approximate, sounds, and sights, and smells that clung somehow to the pavements, to the red brick walls of old tenements, to empty spaces that had once been inhabited by the scuttled fragments of one's youth. Occasionally, you pointed one of these out to your son, but for the most part you walked together silently. One's children are his private clocks, and if your son served to measure just how long it had been, you might yet pause to think that your daughter was already a sophomore on your old college campus, and even that had not survived the years intact. What was Hunter to you, she would call Lehman College, and you would not soon make the adjustment. But then didn't you still, on occasion, refer to the Dodgers as "Brooklyn"?

You continued on, down two long blocks whose landscape was

largely unchanged, but which nonetheless seemed strange now, for it had lost the small details that had somehow defined it. A filling station occupied the vacant lot on which you had played hardball with a taped-up ball and jagged rocks for bases. The dry-cleaning store where you had worked as a delivery boy was boarded up and decorated with graffiti. And where were the initials that, at great risk, you had once carved in the fresh concrete of the sidewalk? At the corner, you looked for the wooden newsstand that had served for so long as a meeting place, but it was gone too, and so was the kosher delicatessen across the street. You started east, up the hill that led to Morris Avenue.

"Where are we going now?" your son asked.

"To the schoolyard," you said, "to Creston."

You knew for certain that Creston, PS 79, was still standing, still open and operating, you knew that for a fact. And as you turned the corner you could see it there in the distance, the curved grill screen that sat atop the roof, the huge crossed-wire fence, perhaps twenty feet high, that surrounded the schoolyard. As you approached, you told your son, probably not for the first time, of some of the games that had been played there and of some of the players who called it home. You described the basket in the southeast corner, where the biggest games were always played, and how it was a shooter's rim, the right side slightly soft and dead to the bounce. There were two intersecting cracks in the pavement just to the right of where the foul line would have been, and you told him how they formed part of the home-court advantage. For you could drive with your head down and when your foot hit those cracks you knew where you were and you could turn and shoot for the dead part of the rim, and you would save that move for when you needed it because after two or three shots your opponent would know to deny you that spot. You told him those stories as you walked down the hill that led to the schoolyard, hoping that there might be a game in progress, that you might get a brief look at the current talent, whose game was certain to be quicker, and very likely better, than yours had been.

It was late in the day now, and the film of dusk was settling into shadows, but you knew that darkness came slowly to the eye of the young. You had played, you remembered, until the streetlights were on, each player a silhouette against the milky light of the street above. So you felt some mild disappointment when you drew even with the fence and found that the schoolyard was empty and nighttime-still, and as you came down the short ramp that led inside from the street, you felt an uneasy sense of desertion about the place, as if it had not just been left untended for the night, but was permanently abandoned. You looked around, and you could see that something was missing, but you did not know what. The eye tends to fill in the anticipated details that the mind might miss, and so it was your son who discerned it before you did.

"Where are the baskets?" he asked.

Yes, that was what was missing. The baskets were gone now; all of them. There were holes in the ground where the supports had been, the cracks still remained in the pavement, but the baskets had been torn from their roots. Basketball was no longer played in the Creston schoolyard.

You did not leave immediately. You waited there a while as if backboards and rims might soon sprout from the concrete. You waited while your mind wandered across the years and familiar figures ran and leaped before your eyes. In the space of perhaps two minutes you reconstructed twenty games and fifty hours of waiting. You resurrected the past, and your youth, and the people who filled it, and then you paced fifteen feet to where the foul line would have been and you focused your eye on an imaginary basket. "Shoot for sides," you could hear a voice say, but the voice was as imaginary as the basket and as illusory as your youth, and then you turned and, together with your son, you walked back up the street. Outside, you stopped for a moment and offered one last glance, for you knew that you would not be passing this way again.

It was a long walk back and you filled the time with a torrent of stories that burst like a flood through the gates of the past. Five years' worth of local folklore were woven into a tight twenty-minute monologue that had no true beginning or end, each vignette strung to the next with the intricate but tenuous logic that one knows only in a dream. It poured forth that way, without interruption, as if what was not said now would be lost forever, and it was necessary to get it all out, to store it in the vaults of youthful memory where it might be held safely for at least another generation. You recounted incidents that you had doubtless told before, others that you did not know you remembered, and some that did not need telling at all because they had become part of history and your son, by now, was almost as familiar with them as you were.

"Were you ever offered money to fix a game?" he asked.

"No," you said.

"How come?"

"Because I would have been a poor investment," you told him. "I wasn't that good."

And then came the question that you were expecting but hoping would not be asked, for there was no way truly to answer it. You had turned it over in your mind a thousand times, imagined it in starkest detail, tried to recall just how much one thousand dollars might have meant to you when you were eighteen years old, and you felt certain that, no, you could not have taken the money. And yet, you knew enough to bless your good fortune, you knew that you had been spared the possibility by the grace of your limited skills, and that virtue's greatest ally was a lack of opportunity.

So you walk away now and leave it all behind. Something indeed has ended, and its loss seems to be beyond measure, for no visible signs remain to mark its passing. It would take a while before you would understand that no monuments are erected to one's youth, and that none is needed. Each generation fashions its own, and they are always sacred, and always temporary, and because they are formed each time from the scraps and pieces that have been left behind by others, they are the truest reminders one can hope for, and the most enduring.

Not many days later, from a terrace overlooking another Bronx schoolyard, your eye is drawn to the hurried tempo of a full-court game. The players are of high school age, and they move up and down the court swiftly, passing the ball with quick precision, firing jump shots on the dead run or feeding the corners on hard drives to the basket. Your point of vantage is from in back of the basket and fourteen stories high, not unreminiscent of your balcony view in the old Madison Square Garden. It is Sunday morning and the school-yard, which is considerably larger than Creston's, is occupied at every corner. There are three baskets in addition to those that form the full court, and there are games going at each of them. Clusters of young-sters, some of them holding basketballs under their arms, are standing in groups of three along the wall behind each basket, waiting to play the winners. It is a scene that evokes the memory of Sunday mornings long ago, and you think that perhaps not so much has changed after all. The center has shifted, but it has held intact against the years. This schoolyard, not much more than ten years old, is not altogether different from your own. It, too, is encircled by a crossed-wire fence, with the baskets at the perimeter, and it offers the added grace of carefully painted foul circles and end lines, and you know that those who play there call it home and that twenty years later one or another might yet return to survey the changes that time has brought.

But now you notice a familiar figure at one of the side baskets. He is the smallest of the six players and he is wearing a short-sleeved sweat shirt with the number thirty-two on the back. He is on defense now, overplaying his taller opponent on the right side, trying to force him away from the basket while at the same time clogging the passing lane. It is a maneuver you had taught him years ago, and he employs it with casual precision. Now a shot is taken and missed, and as the rebound is cleared, he breaks for the head of the circle. There, he takes a quick pass, fakes a move to his left, and then drives the other way. He pulls up just to the right of the foul line, and then suddenly he is in the air, the ball poised lightly above his head, and then his right arm pumps out and with a flick of the wrist the ball leaves his hand and starts its journey upward, a foot, two feet above the rim, and there it hangs for a moment—full moon to a thousand blazing suns—and then begins its descent, not falling but gliding, drifting, skidding as if down a chute aimed at dead center.

Swish, it says.

And you know that as the ball falls to target, the trigger squeezes and on the instant replay of his mind he sees the numbers flash on the scoreboard, and hears the music of the crowd, and as he looks up through a halo of brightly burning lights, something inside him flickers, and it winks its silent tribute to a timeless city dream.

Swish!